You Ain't Done Yet!

Stephen D. Miller, EA, FLMI, CLU, QPA, CFP©

Dedications

There are many people to whom this book should be dedicated, but a few rise above the others and must be recognized. Those include:

1) My wife, Juliann, who has always been my strongest advocate and cheerleader. She kept telling me that I needed to tell these stories. She also purchased a sign that read, "The world is waiting to hear your story" and hung it over my chest of drawers. Each morning I would see this gentle reminder as I got ready for the day. She graduated *summa cum laude* from college, so I am significantly motivated to believe what she says, especially in those incidents when she is paying me a compliment.

2) My friend, Ryan Hervey. He listened to me teach many a class using my stories to get a point across. He is a good friend who has always provided sage wisdom and advice. He studied philosophy in college and then obtained his law degree. He kept telling me that I needed to write some of the stories down before I left this world. He is considerably younger than I, so it seemed important to pay attention. He is a successful financial advisor and I have always marveled at his candor and integrity. Even though he is not an official part of my family, I consider him to be so. We share many philosophies and perspectives. He already uses stories and analogies to illustrate points with his clients. Perhaps someday he will write his stories, too.

3) The many attendees who have heard my presentations and told me that I needed to put my stories in a book, or on an audio CD, or as an online publication. Their constant urging helped to keep me writing, even on those days when the words did not flow easily.

CONTENTS

PREFACE

You are probably wondering how I came up with the title of this book. The title comes from one of the book's chapters. It is a story about work I was doing with a sales rep in the financial services industry, and each time he called me to thank me for helping him develop a solution for a client, I would jokingly respond, "You Ain't Done Yet!" I did this for the humor because of my relationship with the rep, but I was also trying to train him to keep looking for ways to further help his client. The goal was to make him aware of the many needs that this specific client had and to teach him to recognize the many needs other clients might have.

Originally, I had planned to title the book, "The Perfect Question" (another chapter from the book) but after telling many of my stories several times, people who had heard them would point at me when we met later and say, "You ain't done yet." After hearing this enough times I was hit with a revelation: this was the story people remembered most. And, since many of my stories are motivational, I decided it was the message I wanted to convey. No matter where we are in our lives or our careers, we are never done yet. We should always be trying to improve ourselves. We should strive to be better human beings in everything we do.

For more than forty years I have continually learned new things from family members, business associates, religious leaders, instructors, mentors, and even through observation of animals, as you will see in some of my stories. I feel these lessons have been valuable and need to be shared. Intertwined among my stories are my opinions – my two cents – along with a little educational material.

As part of my instructional technique, I tell stories from my experiences. Attendees to my presentations often commented that this educational technique made it easier to learn something, and that they wished I would put these experiences to paper, audio CD, or online book, so they could enjoy them repeatedly. Many work associates said the same thing, so I finally surrendered. This publication is in response to their urgings.

My business background has been diverse. I have been a property manager, a sales representative in the financial services industry, a tax consultant, a corporate employee training and assisting various sectors of the organization, and more. One facet of my activities has been joint work with sales reps and their clients. Many of my stories from these experiences have been included to illustrate a point. In all instances, I have used fictitious names to protect the parties involved from additional scrutiny and contact.

I am hopeful that what I have written will be helpful to you as you grow in your career, but I also hope it will motivate you in all activities of your life. My hope is that you enjoy this collection of articles, and that you have a life filled with blessings and success.

ALI VS. TYSON

My house has five living occupants. I suppose there could be some non-living occupants, but I have lived there more than fifteen years and have yet to see a shimmering apparition in the middle of the night. And, hopefully, any other living residents are simply temporary (e.g. spiders, flies, mosquitoes, etc.).

Besides me, the primary occupants of my house include:

- My wife, Juli, who ascribes to the adage that if one's wife is not happy, then nobody's happy (just kidding);
- A Scotty dog named "Beam me up," (Beam-me, for short);
- A miniature Schnauzer named Bau-Z (Like Jay-Z). We thought he wanted to be a "rapper," but it turns out he is just a "yapper";
- And a yellow Tabby cat named "Schizo," (short for schizophrenic). Schizo can be sitting on the carpet with amber eyes indicating he is at peace, and five minutes later he is jumping six feet in the air at something no one but he can see.

3

This story is about Schizo. It is not about two professional boxers – just two cats who think they are.

A few years ago, I became acutely aware of the animosity Schizo harbors toward all other tomcats in our neighborhood. Actually, I'm probably limiting his degree of hatred, because if there are other tomcats in this universe he hates them, too. His attitude is manifested by his proclivity to seek out tomcats anywhere to do battle with them. He seems to think he is invincible, and this is supported by the fact that his wounds from combat are few. I believe he feels he is like Ali – he can float like a butterfly and sting like a bee.

Only one other cat in the neighborhood is a better combatant than Schizo, and alas, Schizo has permanent scars as evidence. He has a chunk missing from his right ear, which leads me to believe that the other tomcat, who is black and white, believes he may be named Tyson. I don't know his real name but refer to him as Tyson. Tyson is cautious around our house these days.

A few months ago, Tyson bravely chased Schizo into our house through the pet door. Schizo was retreating from battle because Tyson was getting the best of him. Once Tyson entered our house he found out that two cat-hating dogs also lived there. The dogs immediately went into attack mode and "treed" Tyson on top of the kitchen cabinets. The noise was ear-shattering. Two dogs were barking at the top of their lungs. Tyson was hissing back at them but was trapped. That was the night that we discovered that while it may not be possible to herd cats, it is possible to herd one cat. All you need is a squirt gun.

We opened the front door of our house with the dogs locked in the kitchen behind a baby gate, and began to squirt Tyson. He was faced with getting wet or trying to get past two dogs. He chose the latter. He would jump from surface to surface to stay above the dogs. Eventually, he found the open door and scurried from the house. Since then, Tyson has not been back in our home.

Tyson intimidates Schizo enough that Schizo seeks the refuge of home when pursued by Tyson. I'm sure Schizo would not want me to use words like coward to describe him in Tyson's presence, but that does appear to be his demeanor. I'm sure he would prefer the term "cautious." Like most warriors he realizes that sometimes it is necessary to retreat from battle to be able to fight on another day.

I have always found all creatures to be fascinating – both human and otherwise. It's intriguing to watch them and see how they react in different situations. All of them display specific psychological behaviors. What amazes me is the way an animal will plot out a solution to a problem. This is not a characteristic possessed only by humans. The animal may be a monkey trying to figure out how to use a stick to retrieve a banana. Or, it could be a dog analyzing how to get to an animal that has sought shelter under a pile of branches. Perhaps it is a yellow tabby cat named Schizo that is simply trying to go into the backyard to do his "litter box" activity while an invincible cat called Tyson impedes his progress.

To enable our pets to have access to the outdoors, we have installed a pet door. They can exit and enter at will. The pet door is a handy device for us because we do not have to continually open the patio door when our pets need to go outside. For the most part, they employ the door regularly. In the event of a thunderstorm or blizzard, they might not make use of it, but almost 100% of the time, they do.

One day I noticed Schizo sitting at the pet door like he wanted to exit the house, but he was not doing so. Something was making him hesitant. Out of curiosity I looked out the back window and discovered that Tyson was sitting in the middle of the back yard. He is brave enough to enter our yard but knows that he should not enter our house. Schizo obviously needed to use the backyard as his litter box, but Tyson was keeping him inside. Schizo knew he could not beat Tyson when operating from a position of strength, and surely would be more vulnerable from a position of weakness. I was curious to see how he would solve the problem. I decided to watch to see what conclusion he would reach.

As I watched I could tell he was experiencing more discomfiture. He needed to find relief soon. I could almost see his brain at work as it considered alternative solutions. After a few minutes he turned away from the door and went into the other room. Now, I was concerned. Was he not going to go outdoors? Was he going to relieve himself inside? What was he up to?

Now, I need to digress slightly to tell of an activity that is part of every morning in Schizo's life. It is a game that he and our Schnauzer, Bau-Z, play each morning. After being fed, Schizo pounces on Bau-Z. In response Bau-Z chases Schizo around the house. It only lasts a couple of minutes but they both seem to get great enjoyment from the scurrying through chair and table legs. When Schizo feels he has had enough, he simply jumps up on a shelf or piece of furniture. Bau-Z can't make the same jump, so the game ends.

On this particular afternoon, Schizo went into the other room, and I heard him pounce on Bau-Z. Not being conscious of what time of day it was, Bau-Z responded by chasing Schizo – just like he does in the mornings. This time Schizo ran around the kitchen furniture a couple of times with Bau-Z close behind. Then, Schizo went through the pet door to the outside. Bau-Z, who was close to Schizo's tail went through the pet door a microsecond behind. Now, Tyson had two creatures to deal with – a tabby cat AND a Schnauzer (who is not particularly fond of cats). Tyson immediately recognized that his position of power had changed and made a quick retreat. Schizo calmly went to his favorite outdoor restroom spot.

So, why am I telling successful business men and women a story about pets? What can you possibly garner from these anecdotes? What is the moral of this tale, if any? The lesson being portrayed is: If a tabby cat is smart enough to know when to get help, successful sales representatives and employees like you ought to also be.

There's a mentor or manager you can go to who may have previously encountered the same problem you are having and discovered how it could be resolved long ago. Perhaps it's an experienced employee you work with who has had the same problem in his or her past. Asking for help can help you solve the problem faster than if you work it out on your own. Experience is a great teacher, but experience can be slow. First of all, you have to have the experience to learn from it. Secondly, you might have to try several techniques before one works. Getting some help from someone who has experience can often help you resolve the problem more quickly. DON'T LET YOUR PRIDE GET IN THE WAY! ASK FOR HELP! THE PERSON YOU WILL HELP THE MOST IS YOU!

THAT'S AN EASY ONE

I was filling my pickup truck with gasoline when I heard a voice from the adjacent service station bay say, "It's so hot that just blinking is enough physical exercise to make me perspire." I turned to see a distinguished, gray-haired man leaning against his Buick as he refueled his car. He was grinning with satisfaction regarding his comment.

"You got that right," I replied, "It's a typical, steamy August afternoon in eastern Kansas." It felt like you could grab two handfuls of air, compress them within your palms, and water drops would ooze between your fingers and fall to the ground like rain. Local denizens were using many descriptive words: stifling, muggy, sweltering, hot, humid, and suffocating. A few used others: *caliente, humeda y sofocante.* I decided to ride around in my air-conditioned truck and check on some of the apartments I had purchased to gain tax deductions.

I headed off to one of my duplexes. As I pulled to the curb, I was surprised to see Susan working very hard in my yard. Her copper-red hair was matted to her head. Beads of perspiration formed on her forehead, ran down her nose, and dripped onto the board she was nailing to my Mimosa tree. Her green tie-dyed tee-shirt clung to her body like paint. She had to be miserable, but she didn't care. She was on a mission. She was nailing boards to my tree at my duplex with the address 824 on it. The main problem was that she lived in the apartment whose address was 826, and I didn't own that one. Susan was the next door neighbor.

A short explanation about Mimosa trees will be helpful in understanding what was going on. Mimosa trees were brought to the USA from China. They are beautiful trees that bloom with lavender and pink flowers which resemble the coloring in a Peacock's tail. Also, Mimosa branches usually start fairly low to the ground. This particular tree had branches that grew at 45 degree angles starting about two feet from the ground. The low branches made it a huge temptation for the neighborhood children. It was one of the best toys on the block. Apparently, neighborhood children climbed it all the time. And, Susan was dedicated to making their efforts easier.

She was so focused on her task that she did not see me pull up to the curb. Her work was even more challenging because she was holding the claw hammer about three inches from its head. This meant she needed to use many more strokes to sink a nail. Extra hammer strokes on such a hot day increased her perspiration index and amplified the number of salty perspiration beads flowing into her green eyes. She wasn't privy to the information that "just blinking" was already causing a perspiration issue. She continued nailing boards to my tree as I approached.

My shadow passed over her as I approached. Startled, she jerked her head toward me, then relaxed and said, "Hello, Mr. Miller." She seemed slightly concerned, but only slightly. She seemed to brace herself for confrontation, and I sensed a little defiance behind those sweat-filled green eyes. I thought I should pursue our dialogue calmly.

I didn't have any issues with Susan. She was always polite. When I stopped by to work on things at my duplex she usually came over to visit. She was a 33-year old, petite, attractive, single mom, and I found her attention to be flattering – must be a male thing!

I started our conversation. "Susan, what are you doing?"

She stopped hammering, looked up at me from her knees, and said, "I'm nailing boards to your tree."

Now, I may not be the smartest man in the world, but I had already figured that out. "I get that, Susan," I said, "But what I'd like to know is why?"

She sat back on her feet. "I'm making it easier for kids in the neighborhood to climb in it."

"Climbing this tree is not something I want to encourage," I said. "I don't want to risk a kid getting hurt by falling from the tree."

"You're just worried about getting sued," she sighed. "Besides, you can't stop kids from climbing this tree. It's too easy to climb, so they do it all the time."

I admitted, "I am a little concerned about potential legal issues if a child gets hurt falling from the tree, but my primary concern is that I don't want a child to end up with a permanent injury. I had a cousin that fell from a tree when he was eighteen years old and was paralyzed for the rest of his life. I don't want that to happen to anyone else."

"Doesn't matter, Mr. Miller, you can't keep them from climbing this tree."

"I'm sorry, Susan, but I believe that I can stop them."

"But, you can't. It's just too easy to reach the branches. They climb it all the time."

Although I liked Susan, I was becoming annoyed by her attitude. I said, "Susan, the kids can't climb this tree if there is no tree. You see the toolbox on the back of that burgundy pickup right there? There is a chain saw in that toolbox and I can eliminate the lure of this tree by simply cutting it down." (Now that was the last thing I wanted to do because the tree was so beautiful. But, I was befuddled. I didn't know how to keep her from nailing boards to the branches. And, she did have a valid point – the kids already climbed in the tree all the time.)

She pushed me over the edge with her next comment. "I'm gonna go up and down the street and get people to sign a petition to prevent you from removing this tree."

My face turned red with frustration and anger. I'm sure my blood pressure had something to do with my ruddy complexion. I attacked, "Then you'd better start walking, young lady, because this tree will be gone by the time you get back with your petition. Meanwhile, please remove the boards you've already attached to my tree."

I had no intention of cutting down the tree if it could be avoided, but I did not know what to do. What I needed was help. I needed to talk with a friend who might have encountered a similar problem with his rental properties. I needed to talk to Max.

Max owned over a hundred rental units, so I figured he might know what to do. Also, he was a lawyer and would see potential legal problems. He had been a landlord for more than 30 years and had encountered about every problem a landlord could have. I decided to call him. (This was years ago, before cell phones existed, so I went to a small hardware store a couple of blocks away.)

The owner of the hardware store knew me. I bought so many supplies there that we were on a first name basis. He also had the device I needed hanging on the store's wall. (For those of you too young to remember, many years ago many retail stores had a device that you could put a dime into, dial a phone number, and talk to someone on the other end. It was called a pay phone.) I put my dime in and called Max.

Max answered and I told him my problem. "Do you know how I can solve this problem?" I asked.

"That's an easy one," Max chuckled.

"I'm going to have to cut the tree down, right? I was afraid of that. I don't want the legal exposure arising from an injury, but I also don't want to see a little kid get hurt."

"No. It's actually a simpler problem that that," said Max. "Where are you right now, Steve?"

"I'm calling from a hardware store," I explained.

"That makes this even easier to solve," said Max, "You can

13

probably buy what you need right there."

"What do I need, Max?"

"Steve, the hardware store you are in most likely sells a specific tar oil that people paint onto tree trunks, near the base of the tree. It is thought that this will keep insects from climbing the trunk. Purchase some of that and smear it abundantly around the tree's trunk and on its branches. Apply it thickly to each branch. That should solve your problem."

"I'm sorry, Max, but I'm having trouble figuring out how this will keep kids from climbing in my tree."

Max laughed. "You need to look to the end result. There is no detergent that will remove this tar from clothing or shoes. So, if a kid climbs in your tree and gets the tar in his clothes his mom will be very angry with him. She'll say something like, 'If you ever get this stuff on your clothes again, and you'll be grounded for life!' Even if the kid has climbed the tree and got the tar on his clothes once, he will avoid your tree lest he incur mom's wrath again. Now, go ask the store owner to sell you some tar oil."

I purchased a whole 5-gallon can. It was more than I needed but I did as Max told me. I applied it abundantly. It worked. I never had to worry about kids climbing my beautiful Mimosa tree again. I simply applied a little each year. It didn't harm the tree, and it prevented kids from being harmed, too.

So, why am I telling this you this story? I'm going to repeat the message I gave in my previous story. I really want you to learn the value of mentors. You see, on my own I never would have solved my tree problem. Without help I would probably have cut down a beautiful tree simply because it was too enticing to children. But my mentor, Max, had the answer. He knew what to do because of his many years of similar experiences. He knew a simple and inexpensive way to solve my problem.

Right now, you also have access to mentors who can help you with simple solutions to your problems, and you need to take advantage of them while you can. As you have heard me say previously, experience is a great teacher, but experience is slow. Also, you have to have an experience to learn from it. If you never have the experience, you won't know the answer. Near you may be someone who has had the situation you are facing now and who knows a simple way to approach your problem.

If you work in sales, someone with many years of sales experience may quickly help you with a solution for your client. If you are a manager with a problem employee, another manager may give you sound advice for dealing with the problem. You might not always agree with the mentor's suggestion, but when you get the right suggestion you'll know it. Be sure to seek out the advice of your colleagues. You could save a lot of time and be far more productive.

YOU ALWAYS MAKE A SALE,
EVEN WHEN YOU DON'T

When I first started my career in sales, my manager prepared me for the times when a prospect would not buy anything from me. He said, "Sometimes you make the sale. Sometimes you don't. It's mostly a matter of timing. If the client wants your product and has money to buy it, he might. He or she has to choose between spending money on your product or on someone else's. It's your job to help him determine which product is more important to own."

He further illustrated his philosophy by stating, "When a person wants new clothing, he goes to a clothing store. When someone wants a new car, he or she will drive onto a dealer's lot. If there is an interest in buying a new house, a realtor is approached. Until people want something they usually do not seek out a sales person to try to buy it."

"Our products are similar in this way." he continued. "To accumulate money for retirement or a child's education, a person must do without something else they could currently buy with their money. We have an obligation to show people the value of looking toward a goal in the future and doing what is needed now to help them attain that goal."

For the most part, I am inclined to agree with his philosophy. However, I believe his philosophy was somewhat limited. I believe that even in those times that we do not actually convince a prospect to purchase something, we still make a sale. We sell the prospect on our integrity, our product's features and its quality, the service our company provides, how our company stands behind our products, and much more. If handled properly, when the prospect is ready to buy a product we offer, we will be contacted. If handled incorrectly, we won't even be considered at all for future business dealings. Sometimes other business results from the way we conduct ourselves. Even if a prospect is not ready to buy a new product now, he or she may permit us to service the ones already owned.

You have had experiences in your life that illustrate my point. Perhaps you went to a new restaurant in town shortly after it opened and found the food or service to be less than desirable. You then made a decision to not return to that business. If the waiter or waitress who served you was rude, you decided that there were other restaurants you would prefer to patronize instead. In both instances, a sale occurred. You were "sold" on the fact that the business was one you would no longer patronize.

On the other hand, you may have gone to a store to get ideas about new floor coverings for your house and you were treated great. You were not ready to buy flooring when you were there, but the

17

people you talked to were so nice and knowledgeable that you decided that when you were ready to buy the flooring, you would give them the business. A sale was made even though you did not purchase anything at that time. You were sold on what the business offered (quality products, good service, product variety, and integrity, for example). You know you will do business with them in the future.

The title of this short story reflects the personal philosophy I have developed from my years serving clients and their needs. I believe that every time we interact with someone, we make some type of sale. It may not be a product sale now, but it may lead to a product sale in the future. I began to develop this philosophy shortly after I began my sales career. I was 28 years old. Here's how that happened.

Ed and Lois were a young couple with two small children. I had called them and arranged a meeting to discuss a review of their financial products. I wanted to help them see if their financial goals and needs were being adequately addressed. They, like me, were around age 28. When I sat down with them at our appointment I explained how I operated on their behalf.

"Ed and Lois, the first step that I take in this process is referred to as fact-finding," I said. "We talk about what your financial holdings are (where you are right now) and what your goals are (where do you want to go). It's sort of like planning a trip. If you live in Kansas City and want to go to Denver, you have options. You can drive there. You can fly. You can take a train or a bus. Each one has a different cost associated with it, and each option can get you there. Once we have analyzed where you are financially and where you want to go, we will explore different options to get you to your destination."

As I mentioned, this was when I was age 28. It's now many years later and much has changed in the financial planning world. When I was 28, financial planning software did not exist. PCs and Macs did not exist, either. We did all of our sales analyses manually. The fact-finding process was essentially the same as today, but developing solutions took more time. Also, financial product lines were limited. Universal life insurance did not exist. There were only a handful of mutual funds. Annuities had heavy front-end loads so it took a long time to regain the product's investment value. Variable products were still on the horizon. There was no internet (Al Gore was still young). You could not contact people by Facebook. I marvel at how times have changed.

The process we used when I started my career was called "Simple Programming." Through the fact-finding process we determined the income needs for the individuals and their families. Then, we determined what income sources the family had available under varying scenarios (death of an income provider, disability of an income provider, scholarships for college expenses, social security benefits, salaries, etc.). After determining the income shortfalls, if any, under each scenario, we used present-value (mathematical) tables to convert those income needs into equivalent lump-sum figures (i.e., what amount would be needed to provide the income shortfall when used with other available funds). Today, computer software does these same calculations in seconds and produces graphs showing the income shortfalls. Back then, we produced the graphs using graph paper and colored pencils.

After gathering facts from Ed and Lois, I told them I would run the simple programming calculations and return with the results. We scheduled a follow up appointment for a couple of weeks later. Back at my office, I spent the necessary hours producing the reports. I was surprised by the results.

I arrived at Ed and Lois's house on the evening of our appointment. I began, "Ed and Lois, I have completed the analysis you wanted, and I think you will be happy with the results." I discussed the life insurance coverage they owned, the health insurance coverages they had through work, the disability coverage each employer offered, the funds they had set aside for college educations for their children, and how the funds in their life insurance policies and other investments they had would serve them in retirement.

"You have done an excellent job of planning your financial affairs," I said. "In fact, I could not find anything else you need to do. I could talk to you about moving some of your products to other companies, but you already have good products with good companies. If we moved some of your products your financial condition would not improve. You'd essentially be in the same situation you are now. You just need to stay the course. Continue doing what you are doing."

I continued, "Now, this analysis is based on current conditions. If your circumstances change we will need to reassess your goals. We will need to reevaluate your insurance and investments. For example, if you get promotions and your income and lifestyles change, changes in the financial products you own may be needed. Or, if you will have another child, inherit some money, buy a bigger house, or want more retirement income, alterations in your plan may need to be considered. What I usually like to do with clients is complete a new analysis every couple of years. That allows us to see if any gaps have turned up. It also shows us if your investments are still performing well enough to meet your goals. How do you feel about that approach?"

They were shocked. They were certain that I would put pressure on them to buy something or make some change in their plan. After all, that is what had happened every time they had previously met with another financial advisor. That was the understanding they had of insurance sales reps and stock brokers. "Believe me" I said, "If I thought there was a hole in your plan, I would be insisting you take some sort of action. But your plan has no holes at this time. Therefore, you don't need any products I offer. If you had bad products we'd try to make a switch. But you don't. You have excellent products and I cannot really improve your situation."

After I finished explaining my analysis, it was my turn to be shocked. Until this meeting with Ed and Lois I had not encountered a young couple whose financial objectives were being met so well. Lois said, "Mr. Miller, what you just did for us…could you also do that for our family and friends?"

I replied, "I address all my clients' needs the same way that I have addressed yours. I perform an analysis based on the facts provided. If there are gaps I illustrate them. Where there are no gaps, or I cannot improve their position, I tell them."

I waited for Lois to speak. "Would it be okay if we gave you the names of some people we would like you to contact? We really think they could use your help." (I was going to ask for referrals anyway, but Lois brought it up). This was a new experience for me.

"That would be great," I said.

She grabbed a pencil and a tablet (paper – iPads and Surfaces had not been invented) and her phone book and started writing. She would write down a name and then look up the phone number associated with the name. She included family and friends on her list. She provided around twenty names. Then she added, "Mr. Miller, would it be okay if we called these people to let them know that you will be calling them?" I was almost speechless (a condition most people do not associate with me).

"I think that would be wonderful, Lois. I promise I will follow up with them." I tried not to look too excited as I took her list. I had never had an experience like that. I had not made a product sale with them, but, I obviously had made some type of sale. I had convinced them that I was the type of financial advisor they would want their family and friends to meet. That was the first situation that taught me that even if you don't make a sale, you make a sale.

I also learned another important rule from this experience. People will tell their friends about you. If you treat them well, they'll tell their friends about you. If you cheat them, they'll tell their friends about you. What they tell their friends about you is totally in your control.

Thirty years later, I was still learning that you always make a sale, even when you don't make a sale. Let me explain.

I had been called in to help one of my financial planning friends with one of his cases. He had done a seminar for an employee group, and one of the attendees had approached him after the meeting. Helen was age 62 and wanted to know if she had enough money to retire. On the surface it looked like she could. She had more than $650,000 in her 401(k) plan. We met with her and gathered the information we needed to run a financial plan. We explained that it was a two-step process and we would meet again after running the numbers. This time I was able to perform the calculations using computer software. Instead of hours, it took only around one hour. As part of the process, I ran several "what if" scenarios.

I wanted Helen to feel comfortable that her money would last throughout her retirement. I wanted her to feel assured that her money would last as long as she lived. Helen had a few demands that made it challenging for me to say that. A year before our meeting, Helen had purchased a larger house on her block. Her mortgage payments had gone up quite a bit but she wanted to keep this house. She did not want something smaller. She also indicated that she wanted to travel when she retired and gave us an estimate of what she thought it would cost.

She was generous with her family and gave them gifts every year. She wanted to keep doing that. She also wanted to continue supporting her favorite charity that cared for animals. I ran the numbers for her to see what her future would look like after including her conditions.

Hers was a very tempting case because she had $650,000 to rollover. It would have been so easy to tell her that her money would surely last throughout her retirement. I could have made an easy sale and made an easy commission (split with the planner who brought me to the case). But, I wanted her to be able to sleep at night. I wanted her to know her money would last. I suspect that there are financial advisors who would have done the rollover before she could change her mind without checking to make sure her funds were adequate. For them, the commission would have been a key motivating factor. Instead, I completed various scenarios for her.

When we (the financial planner and I) called to set up the follow up appointment, she said, "Would it be okay if my brother came to our meeting? He's better at finances than I, and I would appreciate his input."

Throughout my career I have often had similar requests from clients and prospects. Most people have a family member, close friend, accountant, or attorney whose opinion they value. I assured her that we would be honored to have her brother attend.

We faced her at the table. The financial planner who found the client was to my left. Her brother was to her right. I began the explanation of the numbers I had produced. Because she had notified me her brother would be there, I made an extra copy of my materials for him. I explained that based on the computer results her money would easily last into her 80s (if she continued earning 6% or more from her investments and if she decided to retire now). I also explained that if she earned a lower return the money would not last as long. However, it would last into her late 70s. If she earned only 4%, the timeline was shorter.

My analysis showed that if she waited until she was 65 to retire (just three more years), she would pick up more retirement income from all of her sources. Her social security income would be higher. She would have three more years to put more money away into her 401(k) (which meant it should provide more retirement income). The employer's defined benefit pension plan would provide her a higher income because she would be older. The calculations revealed that even with inflation of 3% throughout retirement, her money would last for her lifetime, even if she only earned a 4% return. Her income, if she waited three more years to retire would allow her to do everything she wanted to do in retirement. I explained that the choice was hers. If she decided to retire now, we would help her with a slightly more aggressive investment plan to try to get higher earnings. Or, she could wait three more years to retire and the numbers would "sing" even if she had conservative investments. She decided to wait three more years to retire.

I could tell that the sales rep that had brought me to the case was disappointed. He probably had already thought about how he was going to spend his share of the commission from the $650,000 rollover. However, his disappointment slipped away, when the brother spoke.

"Would you be able to do this kind of analysis for me?" The brother asked.

He was around the same age as his sister, so I figured he wanted to try to retire, as well. "We'd be happy to run an analysis for you. May I ask what assets you have?"

He didn't hesitate to answer. I think he was impressed that we didn't just try to rollover his sister's money without explaining the challenges she would face. "Right now, my assets are primarily in cash. But, I need to hold some money back to pay the taxes that resulted from the sale of the property that generated this cash."

I responded, "We would build the tax calculation into your analysis so we would know what amount is left to help fund your retirement. May I ask what type of property was sold to generate the cash?"

He smirked a little when he answered. "It came from the sale of my small hotel chain."

You always make a sale, even when you don't!

IT'S NOT ABOUT FEATURES

I stared at the screen of my laptop computer as I waited for it to finish processing my business software. It was taking a long time. That was common. I knew that the graphics and calculations in the programs I was using had expanded beyond my computer's capabilities. In fact, I kept magazines and books on my desk to read as calculations were being performed. Even though I fostered thoughts of frugality, I knew it was time to buy a new laptop.

About 500 yards from my home is a national brand electronics store. I decided to start there first. Not being conversant in computer lingo, I expected to be intimidated by the floor representative that helped me, but alas, it was something that needed to be pursued. The computers were located at the back of the store so I walked past many other items I'd rather shop for and stood in front of the laptops. I didn't know where to begin. There were about sixteen units to consider.

In only a couple of minutes, a young store clerk approached. He looked about 17 years old. I took comfort in the thought that he would know a lot about computers. It seems that the knowledge one has about computers is inversely proportionate to one's age. The younger a person is, the more he or she knows about computers. *If this clerk were 12 years old he would know even more about computers*, I thought.

The young man, Brian, spoke first. "How may I help you?" he asked.

I explained my plight regarding my laptop's slow processing time.

"How old is your laptop?" He inquired.

"About 5 or 6 years." I replied.

"You definitely should consider a new computer." He said. "Software has been expanding so fast that older computers simply cannot process programs efficiently. You usually notice this problem as early as two years after you put a computer in service. You're almost three times that length of time. Would you prefer a desktop computer or a laptop?"

"I need something portable because I often take the computer with me when I see clients. That way I can change any input amounts that have changed since my initial fact-finding interview."

"Okay. You need a laptop. Let's look at some of our options." He moved to the left side of the laptops, which were on two levels, and began to describe the various features of each computer. I was amazed at how many details he remembered about each one, especially since every year new models came out and the features changed. He was obviously passionate about computers.

As he started his explanation of each brand and model, and its capabilities, I was reminded of the Charlie Brown specials on television. His presentation became a drone to me. It seemed like all I was hearing was, "Wah Wah Wah!" If I did know a computer term he was using, I didn't know how it applied to my computer needs.

He explained the features of each laptop he had. He talked about: Core processors, Gigahertz processing speeds, Solid state drive options, video partitioning and editing capabilities, gaming use, RAM capacity, advanced graphics capabilities, pixel clarity, battery life, and more. When he had finished giving the details of his last laptop, I heard myself say to Brian the same thing you will hear from your clients when you unload the details of your product and provide an abundance of confusion. I said, "Brian, I really appreciate the details you've given me. It's a lot for me to absorb right now. I only live a few hundred yards from here so what I am going to do is go home and think about which computer I need. After I decide, I'll be back."

Why did I tell Brian I wanted to think about it? Because my pride would not let me say, "I can't make a decision right now because I'm too stupid to understand what you said." He really knew a lot about computers, but he assumed that I knew more about them than I did. Another computer wizard would have undoubtedly appreciated his monologue about each unit, but it did not assist me in making a decision. He needed to make the presentation fit my skill level. He didn't. So, I still needed a new computer, but I didn't know what to buy.

There was another national chain electronics store a couple of miles away so I decided to go there. Again, the laptops were at the back of the store. By putting them at the back I suspect impulse buying occurs. I saw many things I wanted to buy as I walked toward the computers.

It looked like this store had essentially the same brands and models as the first store. As I stared at the various models a sales representative approached. But this time the sales rep appeared to be about 35 years old. Remembering my axiom that computer knowledge is inversely connected to age, I wondered just how helpful he would be.

He started with the familiar retail question, "How may I help you?"

Again, I explained my need for speed. But this time the approach was different.

He asked several questions: "How will you be using the computer? Will you need portability? Will you use it for games? Will you be using it to edit home videos? Will you be using it primarily for business (e.g., word processing, spreadsheets? etc.)?

I answered all of his questions. When I was through, he said, "You either need this laptop (as he pointed to the one near the lower left corner) or this one (as he pointed to one near the middle of the upper shelf."

"How is it that you can tell which one I need?" I inquired.

"Based on the parameters of use that you gave me either of these will be the most efficient for you. Some of the others have different capabilities that you don't need and are more expensive, so why pay for the features you don't require? Either of these two will accomplish what you need?" He smiled and waited for my response.

I noticed that the laptop on the second shelf was $600 more than the one on the lower shelf. My thriftiness prevailed. "Why would I spend $600 more on that one?"

He nodded. "I knew you would ask that question. I certainly would." He went on, "The one that costs more has much more memory capability. In fact, we can expand its memory considerably. That way you won't need another new computer as soon. The cheaper one will probably only give you about two years of efficient service and then software will reduce its speed. The more expensive one will probably get you four years before you need to consider a new laptop."

"I'll take the more expensive one." I said. I left the second store that day with a new laptop computer. I also felt relief that I would not need to talk to another computer salesman for four years.

Do you see the difference between the two sales representatives? One explained product features. The other matched my needs with the benefits I sought. Not every purchase we make is based on the benefits we receive from a product, but most purchases are based on them.

In my experience as a financial planner, I rarely had clients ask me about product features. Oh sure, they want to know some of the features like liquidity, return rates, etc., but the real questions they ask are: Can you help me build a college fund for my child? Can you help me acquire enough money for retirement? Can you help me take care of my family if I die or become disabled? These are the benefits they seek. First and foremost, this is what they want. Features become secondary to the goal. You still need to know the features of your products to know which ones fit the client's risk tolerance and suitability. Knowing a product's features helps you guide a client to the right choice. Sometimes, you will need to give the client a couple of options, explain the features, and let the client decide. But remember, the first thing that must be ascertained is what benefit the client seeks.

Whatever your occupation, discovering the benefit desired improves your success. If you sell cars, you need to know if the client needs to be able to haul several people, or needs off-road capabilities, or needs to tow a camper, and the like. You only find this out by asking questions. Ask your client what he or she needs the vehicle to accomplish.

If you are an accountant you will need to find out what your client wants. Does he/she want you to do all of the accounting or just audit the books? After explaining your services your client may choose more, but you need to start by discovering the benefits your client seeks.

Remember, it's not really about your product's features. First it's about the benefits your client wants to receive. Let your client know you want to find the right match for them and start asking questions. When the client senses your sincerity they'll open up to you. You'll be in a better situation to match your services or products to their needs.

TWO STEPS OF SELLING

Sometimes you encounter something in this life that is just too good to be true. That's what Juli was for me. She stood five-nine, had brown hair with streaks of auburn, and had a model's figure (in fact, she had been a model). Under her dark brown eyes was a sparkle revealing an intelligence that others may not have recognized. I could not take my eyes off of her. Then, neither could any of the other guys in the church singles group to which we belonged. Even today, after twenty-five years, I have trouble not staring at her. (If she reads this, I'll be in trouble – it'll probably cost me another pair of shoes). But, the true icing on the cake is that we are intellectually matched. We have the same philosophies, religious beliefs, political views, love of music, love of animals, and more.

It was twenty-five years ago when we met. But, after visiting with her for a few minutes I felt like I had known her forever. I knew I had been searching for her for forty-four years. I knew I needed to employ every sales skill I possessed to convince her to go out with me.

Fortunately, I organized many of the outings for our singles group, so this gave me the opportunity to call her often and let her know the events the group would undertake (e.g., plays, movies, sporting events, etc.). In one of our conversations I asked her if she wanted to go with me to a new jazz restaurant in town, and she accepted. I made sure she knew that this was not a singles group outing – it would just be the two of us. That was the beginning of a great relationship. (Today, she is my wife and has been for more than twenty years).

When I first met Juli, she was a bookkeeper at a company that sold and serviced forklifts. She was very skilled as a bookkeeper. She knew the cost of everything, the profit margins of the products they sold, had a great relationship with customers, and could even collect money on accounts that were in arrears where third-party collection companies had failed. She was a valuable asset to her company. But, her job at the company did not make her feel fulfilled.

When I met her she did not have a college degree. (Eventually she graduated *summa cum laude* with a Business Degree). After dating a few months she asked me, "What type of career do you think I should pursue?"

I responded, "You are intelligent and attractive. You can be anything you want. However, you would be very good as an attorney or a sales representative."

She wanted more information. "Why do you say that?"

I replied, "Because you like to argue, and you have to win." (I'm still in trouble over that statement. Statistics would show that I have not won too many "debates" in our house, so my comment was accurate.)

"So, how do I become an attorney?" Her question was serious as she stared at me, awaiting my answer.

I gave her an honest answer. "That'll take a little time. The first thing you would need is a college degree. After that, you would need to be accepted to law school and complete the program to get your Juris Doctorate. It will take you about seven years. Then, you will need to pass the bar if you intend to practice law."

"That sounds like a long time," she said. "How do I become a sales representative?"

"To be a sales rep, you simply need to get someone to hire you. Figure out what products you want to sell and apply for positions with companies selling those products. Then you work hard, follow the training program they give you, ask for advice from other reps, and start seeing prospects. Choose a product field that you find interesting and believe in. It's always easier to sell something you believe in."

She pondered what I had said and asked, "What do you think I would be able to sell?"

"How do you feel about selling forklifts? It's not a product line sold by many women, but if you learn the product you should have no trouble getting in to see owners and officers of companies that use them. And, you already know the finances connected with the products your company sells. You know about purchase and lease options. You know how much profit the company needs to cover costs. You're aware of the warranty programs, etc. You probably know more about the financial side of your company's products than most of the other sales reps. You also know about the costs of parts and repairs for forklifts brought to your company for service. I think you should approach your company about letting you sell their forklifts."

It was evident that she was thinking about what I had said. "It sounds interesting, but I know what my company will say. They'll say that there are no women selling forklifts and won't give me the chance to try. What'll I do if they say that?"

"You've told me that they have a lot of turnover of sales reps. You've also mentioned that the company is always looking for a new sales rep to replace one who has not been successful. My suggestion is that you be persistent. Every time a sales rep fails, remind them again that you'd like to give it a try."

She was cautious. This was a new area of thought for her. "So, what happens if I can't make it as a sales rep? What do I do then?"

"Well, you are an excellent bookkeeper. You can easily return to that career path. But, if you work hard, I don't see you failing. You have too much drive for that. I think you will be very successful if they give you a chance. I'm not trying to push you to do something you don't want to do, but at this point, I don't think you have anything to lose. The risk is small and the rewards can be great. The decision is yours. As the adage goes, the ball is in your court."

A couple of months passed and one of the company's recently

hired sales reps was laid off. He just had not produced the results needed to justify his employment. Juli approached the sales manager. "I'd like to apply for the sales rep position that just opened," she said.

The sales manager approached the conversation with caution. "Do you have any sales experience?" he asked.

"I've never sold forklifts, but I've been involved in sales. I helped sell real estate a few years ago. I promoted a bar and restaurant in which I was a partial owner. And, I worked with a local political candidate and got her elected. I'm not afraid to approach prospects and explain the value of a product I am selling." She waited for his response.

It was clear that he did not know how to respond. Finally, he leaned across his desk. "Well, Juli, I appreciate your interest in the job, but right now there are no women selling forklift products. It's just not a field where women have credibility."

She kept her composure. "A few years ago there were a lot of professions in which women were not thought of as viable candidates. Today, women are abundant in those positions. I think this is a field where women can excel, and I'd like a chance to try it." She pointed out all of the knowledge she possessed about the company and its products and how that knowledge would help her sell its products.

He leaned back in his chair. "Well Juli, I appreciate your interest and drive. I'll definitely consider you for the spot." A couple of weeks later, they hired a man for the sales rep position. She suspected they would, but decided not to say anything. She decided she would be patient.

A few more months passed. Another sales rep had been terminated for lack of production. She approached the sales manager again. Her conversation paralleled the one she had before. She was told that she would be considered for the job, but again, the company hired a male sales rep. While somewhat upset about the way the company was handling her request, she decided to remain patient and positive.

More time passed and another male sales rep was laid off for lack of production. Again, she approached the sales manager. Again, the conversation was almost identical to the previous ones they'd had. She knew what the outcome would be. They hired another male sales rep.

More than a year had transpired when the next sales rep was terminated for lack of production. Juli approached the sales manager again and expressed her interest in trying to sell the company's products.

"I knew you would be here again," he said. "Juli, the world hasn't changed since the last time we talked. This is still a field dominated by male sales reps. Women are just not selling forklifts."

She looked at him and decided to take a bold approach. "Based on the number of male sales reps you've terminated in the last eighteen months for lack of production, I'd say there are not many men selling them either! Perhaps the reason women are not selling forklifts is that they are not given the opportunity. It seems like a small risk for you to try me out for the job. Or, you could simply hire another male sales rep that'll probably fail."

She had a point. He hired men to sell forklifts all the time and ended up firing most of them. *I guess she couldn't do much worse than they,* he thought. He liked her moxie. He said, "Juli, you make a lot of good points. I think we will give you a chance. We're going to move you to a sales position. Give us a couple weeks to find a bookkeeping replacement for you. Then, we'll begin training you to sell forklifts."

When she got home she wasted no time telling me she was going to be a forklift sales rep. "Now what do I do?" she asked.

"The first thing you need to do is study," I said. "You need to learn as much as you can about the products your company sells. They'll teach you what their product's strong points are compared to the competition. They will give you an introduction to what to say when you encounter resistance. Then, you will need to begin approaching companies that use forklifts. Forklift sales, like many products, will depend on timing and keeping your company information in front of the prospect. If they have budgeted for a new forklift they'll be more receptive. If the old forklift is beginning to cost more in repairs than a new one would, they will listen more closely. In some instances it may take many months before they act. In others, they may act immediately. Just keep letting them know you are available to help."

"But, what is the key to sales success?" she asked. "Is there a special secret that helps people succeed in sales?"

"Basically, selling consists of two steps," I said. "Step one is that you have to go see somebody. In other words there has to be contact with a potential buyer. You can send them a brochure. You can call them. You can stop by to see them. But, until you actually have contact with a decision-maker no sale is going to happen. The second step is that you have to ask the decision-maker to buy your product. It doesn't matter what you are selling, all sales activities involve these two steps. The more activity you have doing these, the more success you will have."

I continued, "In the early stages of your sales career you will encounter objections that you have not heard before. You won't know what to say. Don't worry. You'll have to tell the prospect that you will get back to them with the answer they seek. Then, you'll ask one of the successful sales reps how they would respond to the objection. The next time you hear that objection you'll know what to say, because you have already had that experience. In time, you will know what to say for most objections you encounter. Just be honest with the prospect. Prospects know that no one has all the answers. They, too, get questions every day that they have to research about the products and services they offer. Your prospect will be patient in most cases because he or she needs accurate information to make the right decision about your products. You will do well if you just recognize that you are in a learning curve and apply yourself to gain the knowledge you need.

She began the arduous task of studying product brochures and asking mechanics about the products the company offered. She became so knowledgeable about the forklifts they offered that she could stand on the other side of a row in a lumberyard and tell the brand of forklift being used by its sound alone.

To help her learn more about selling I purchased motivational CDs and CDs on selling (e.g., Zig Ziglar, Napolean Hill, etc.), and she would listen to them in her car as she traveled to appointments. She organized her time to produce maximum results. Three years after she started selling forklifts, she was among the top sales reps in her company. Even the competitor sales reps knew who she was because she was hurting their sales. When she arrived at the company of a potential prospect, she fell into the habit of introducing herself to everyone in the lobby. If she arrived at a company when a competitor sales rep was there and tried to introduce herself to him, the rep would often say, "You don't need to introduce yourself. I already know who you are."

She was always prospecting. If we went to a party and she was introduced to someone she did not know, she would ask the new acquaintance where he or she worked. If his or her company appeared to be a manufacturing, shipping, or warehouse entity, she would ask if the company used forklifts. If the person said his or her company did she would briefly describe what she did and ask if she could set up a time the next week to show how her company's products might be helpful. If we drove by a business building she would ask me to pull around back to see if there were forklift pallets. If there were, she would make a note to call on the business the next week.

Her sales success caught the attention of management. Here was a woman outselling a lot of men in an industry usually dominated by men. They wanted to know how she was doing it. They wanted to make sure her activities were ethical. She was called into the owner's office.

"Juli," said the owner, "we are proud of the job you are doing and we want to know why you are so successful, when some of our reps seem to struggle. Would you be willing to share how you've had such great success?"

She was a little disturbed by the question. She wondered if the owner had ever called his most successful sales rep in to the office to ask this question. She responded, "I'll be happy to help, but I need you to do a little homework. Today is Monday. I'll answer your question on Friday, if you will gather information from the other sales reps before our meeting. I'm sure their answers will shed light on why I am so successful. Is that acceptable?

"I think that's a great idea. We want our other reps to be successful, too. What would you like me to do?"

"All you need to do is ask them a simple question. Ask them how many inventory or materials handling companies each rep calls on in a week. Once you have that answer, we'll talk about my approach." He agreed and they set up a meeting for Friday afternoon.

It was two o'clock PM on Friday, and Juli entered the owner's office. "Do you have my answer as to why you are so successful?"

"I do," she answered. "Have you done the homework I asked you to do?"

He nodded affirmatively. "I called the sales reps in and asked them how many companies they called on in a week."

"What did the reps say?" she asked.

"Each one had a slightly different answer, but depending on the number of existing clients that required ongoing service from the rep, the number was between 12 and 20 per week. I think that's a pretty normal number among sales reps in our industry. Is that what you were looking for?"

"It's perfect," she said, "and it's what I suspected. I think you are correct. Those are probably accurate statistics for sales reps in our industry. But, my statistics are a little different. When possible, I try to get some of the office personnel here to follow up on phone calls from clients. They simply call the customer and let them know that my schedule for the day limits my ability to contact them for a while. They ask the client if they can be of service. Many times they can, and that lets me continue calling on prospects. If the customer feels he or she must talk to me, they let the customer know that I'll be calling in to check on what service needs to be provided. Most the time the customer appreciates not having to wait until I'm available. The other sales reps probably try to handle all the follow up service themselves. They often play phone tag several times before they make contact. This approach limits the time they have available to call on new prospects."

She continued, "Because I have more time to call on new prospects, I can. Each morning when I leave for the office it is my goal to contact at least 20 new companies that day. I don't always make that goal, but I sure try. Sometimes, my contact is only to drop off a brochure and let them know I will follow up to see if we can help them with any inventory handling issues. Other times, I actually get to talk to a decision maker for a few minutes. If I do not have a scheduled appointment, I introduce myself to the new prospect. I let them know what our company does and how we can help. I let them know that we offer new forklifts, but I also let them know we offer used forklifts, mechanical services, parts and tires."

"So, the main reason I am having greater success than some sales reps is that I am simply seeing more prospects than they. Seeing more people usually presents more sales opportunities. It's all about efficient activity."

A few days later the owner told the rest of the reps what Juli was doing - just like I'm telling you now. You will be more successful if you have more efficient activity. It's not just activity. If you are seeing a lot of people and not making sales, it might be because you are approaching people who are not good prospects for your product. You need to decide who fits your products. You need to determine how your product benefits them and find ways to show them. Then, you need to ask them to purchase what you offer.

So, even if you had a good year last year, I'm sure you want a better one this year. I know your manager and your company wants you to have a better year. So, what's the answer to having a better year? Remember, it actually involves two steps: 1) Go see more people, and; 2) Ask them to buy the benefit your product offers from you!

IT'S ALL ABOUT LISTENING

Several years ago I experienced the big "D." No, not Diabetes, it was that other thing that Tammy Wynette sang about, a D-I-V-O-R-C-E. I came home from a lousy day at work and discovered that I had less furniture than when I left for work that morning. That was my first sign.

My neighbor strode across the street and rang the doorbell. When I opened the door he asked, "Are you guys moving?"

"No." I responded. "But, I think my wife is."

Now, from the title of this chapter you might think this is an article about how I should have been a better listener in my marriage to make it work. But, alas, it isn't. There are just some things that listening can't fix. However, there are other situations where better listening can greatly improve our relationships. This is especially true in business. Good listening usually helps in our personal relationships, too. I'll write more about this a little later.

Shortly after the court decision, I moved to Kansas City to take a new job. It didn't take long before I knew that I needed to get a newer car. The one I was driving was beginning to display a few problems. One notable problem was that it had developed a leak around the front windshield as a result of a collision with a deer. The auto body shop could not stop the leak. I knew I needed a new car because my olfactory senses were attacked by the aroma of mold every time I opened a car door. I was embarrassed to offer a ride to friends or new acquaintances.

I had a pretty good idea of what I wanted. I had narrowed my picks down to three vehicles because they offered the most utility to me. Since I regularly played music in contemporary church services, and played at some private parties, I needed a car with some cargo space. However, being newly singled, I also wanted a car that was a little sporty. I had delusions of young women eagerly pursuing me and felt they should ride in style.

I had decided that I needed either a Ford Probe (tells you how long ago this was), a Nissan 240SX, or a Dodge Daytona. All of these vehicles were sporty and had hatchbacks. The hatchback design gave me easily accessible cargo room for hauling musical equipment. With my goal established I headed to a large automobile dealership a few miles from my apartment.

I had probably been on the dealer parking lot for almost one and one-half minutes before a salesman greeted me. In fact, I think I still had one leg in the car when he arrived. "How may I help you?" He asked. From that question I knew he had worked in retail sales for a while and had received training in selling techniques.

You see, if you simply ask a customer, "May I help you?" you may hear the client say he or she is just looking. Or they might simply say "no." By adding the word "How" to the question some customers may indicate what they are seeking to find. It doesn't always work, but it improves a sales reps chance of getting more information.

I answered the salesman's question. "I'm looking for one of these three cars." I described why I needed one of these particular models while he nodded affirmatively. After a few minutes he approached me with keys in his right hand, and I followed him to a line of cars a hundred feet away.

"We're going to take this one for a drive," he said as he pointed at a dark blue Buick Regal. I thought that we might be driving it to another lot where he would show me one of the three cars I had specified. He handed me the keys and indicated I should drive. As I drove he pointed at streets I should take. A few minutes later, he had taken me in a circle and we were back at the parking lot. He took the keys and showed me how the backseat folded to make more cargo space. The trunk and the back seat offered quite a bit of cargo room, but not enough for some of my musical equipment. He asked me how I liked the Buick.

Trying to remain polite, I asked, "Do you remember that I specified that I needed a hatchback for more cargo area and for ease of entry?"

"This car has a lot of cargo space," he said almost indignantly.

"It does have some nice cargo room, but it is not easily accessible. Also, it's not very sporty."

"He said, "Let me get another set of keys for a different car to try out."

I waited until he returned with the keys and followed him a little farther down the lot. He stopped behind a Honda CRX. Now, I don't know if you remember what the CRX looked like, but I think the desk in my office was bigger than this car model. It was cute, but a couple of my PA speakers would not have begun to fit inside. I explained this to him. "He looked at me and said, "But, it is a hatchback."

At this point my blood pressure is a little higher than when our conversation started. "Were you listening when I told you the three cars that I had chosen as acceptable for my needs?"

"I was," he responded, "but we don't have any of those right now." He shrugged as though that would make a difference.

"Do you ever get any of these models on your lot?" I was working to maintain my composure.

"We get them in all the time. We just don't have any right now."

I continued. "Well, at this time you are simply wasting your time and my time. You haven't shown me anything I will buy. I spent a lot of time narrowing down the type of car I need. You could be wasting some other customer's time. Or, maybe you could actually be making a sale to another customer. I'm just about ready to leave, but if I go to another dealer, I'll probably be treated the same way. So, I'll make a deal with you. If you promise to call me when you get one of these cars on your lot, I won't go shopping at another dealer. I've got reliable transportation right now. I'm just wanting something a little sportier that offers as much function as my current car. I can wait as long as 6 months until you get one of these on your lot."

He agreed to call me when one of these models showed up. I indicated that I was also looking for a low mileage car. After the big "D" I really did not feel I could afford a new car. I needed time to rebuild my finances again. I understand there are other people who have found themselves in similar financial circumstances after the big "D." I think the salesman was one of them.

I went back to my regular schedule – going to work and back to my apartment. I waited for the salesman to call. Fortunately, it only took about 10 days. I needed a car that smelled better.

I answered the phone and he said, "I've got your car."

Because of the visit I had at the lot, I wasn't sure what he had for me. "What it is?" I inquired.

He seemed quite proud of the car he wanted to show me. "It's a white, Dodge Daytona. It's loaded and only has 11,000 miles on it." I made the arrangement to meet him after work. It was a Friday so I knew I would get off work in time.

As I drove onto the dealer's lot, I could see the Daytona. It was beautiful. Newly waxed, it glistened brightly in the sunlight. Over the rear window were black louvers. Special mag wheels with fat tires stood out, giving it a sleek design. It looked like it was racing even when it was standing still. Now, I had a dilemma. I had to pretend I didn't want the car as spittle drooled down my cheek. I needed to negotiate a good price. I knew that was going to be hard because I really wanted the car. The salesman told me there were only three like it in a tri-state area.

We took it for a ride. We agreed on a price, and I bought it. He even gave me a good trade-in value. The smell of mildew was not going to keep him from getting his commission. When the transaction was completed, I gave the salesman a little reminder about how much easier it is to sell a car when you listen to the customer. He could have saved himself a couple of hours of showing me the wrong cars the first time I was there. Who knows? In that amount of time he might have sold a car to someone else. You need to remember this when dealing with your customers. They might not always know what they want like I did, but they know what the end result needs to be. You can find this out by asking the "perfect" question. (See the chapter with this title.)

I don't want to disparage the salesman's attempt to sell me a car when he did not have any models I wanted. He could have helped the situation by asking, "Would it be okay if I showed you a couple of other cars that might be suitable for your needs? While we get those models in all the time, we don't have any right now." I probably would have given him permission. It worked out well for him that time because I still bought a car, but many customers would simply have left and gone to another dealer.

I drove the Daytona for a couple of days. When most of us get a new car we want to drive it around, and I did. I'm sure my head stood more proudly on my shoulders as I paraded my car throughout my neighborhood. After a couple of days I needed to fill with gas.

I pulled up to the pump, got out, inserted the nozzle, and began to add fuel. In the next bay was a young woman that I guessed to be

51

around 26 years old. She walked over and said, "Wow, that is one pretty car!"

I smiled at her and said thank you.

She added, "This might seem a little forward, but is there any chance I could go for a ride in it?" (Honestly, that really happened. It wasn't a dream that I was having.) I told her I would be happy to give her a ride and worked out the details, since I didn't know her.

She drove her car to one of the parking spots at the station. She got out, walked to the passenger side of the car, and got in. I suspect I had a big grin on my face, because I was thinking: I wonder if this would have happened if I had purchased the Regal or the CRX.

You need to find out what your customer wants, whatever your product is. It's okay to suggest another alternative. Sometimes you can upgrade the customer to another product for the same price. Or, you can show them benefits from a different product that go beyond what they had in mind. Just be sensitive to their desires. Be polite. Respect their views, and ask if you can show them something else. You might be having a sale on a particular product line that would help to influence their decision. You might have a different product that has a lot more features for the same price. I can't dwell on this enough. Ask questions. See what they are willing to spend. Discover what needs they have. Design the solution to fit their desires. Hear what they say when they describe what they want. Your goal should always be customer satisfaction.

SHOW YOUR INVENTORY

In the chapter, "It's All About Listening", I admonished a car salesman for showing me inventory that did not meet my objectives. I still stand by this position, but for the most part, I think a good salesman will attempt to sell a product he/she has if he doesn't have the model a customer wants. The salesman needs to ask the customer if it would be okay to show some alternative products that might work. Customers don't always know what's available, and a salesman can open up their minds by showing a new product or an alternative product.

If you are selling a technological product this happens all the time. It's happened to me. There have been times that I went looking for a new cell phone, only to discover there were more options than I thought. Fortunately, the sales person mentioned there were some new options available, if I cared to see them. Often, I've purchased something different than what I entered the store to buy.

I recall going to a car dealer with the goal of buying a new car. I told the sales person that I wanted a particular model in white. He told me that he did not have that color in stock at the moment, but could get it for me. "However," he said, "I do have that model in stock in silver. You could test drive it to make sure that it's the model you want. If you would be interested in considering the silver color, I could put you in to that model today." I came onto the lot seeking a white car but drove off the proud owner of a silver one.

One time I went to my favorite men's clothiers and told my regular salesman, who would call me when the store had a sale or got a new item in, that I wanted a new suit in a dark shade of green. He said, "I know you'd look good in that color, and I can get it for you, but have you ever considered a dark shade of brown? With your skin tone I believe that a dark brown suit would look good on you. It doesn't cost anything to try it on. If you like it, you will be adding another color to your wardrobe. Also, you can wear the brown suit while you wait for the green one you want to arrive." I ended up buying the brown suit, too.

Because I was a musician, I often visited music stores to shop for new equipment. This is an affliction most musicians have. In this technological age there are always new devices that produce different sounds and musicians always want to stay up to date on them. Guitars now have electronics that change the sounds they produce. One time I went in to a music store to buy a Gibson ES335 guitar (like BB King played) and left the store with a new Gibson Les Paul. The salesman pointed out that they both had similar pickups and a fat sound, but for certain rock songs the Les Paul produced less feedback. The hollow body of the 335 could cause the notes to last a little too long in certain songs.

My wife had a name-brand vacuum sweeper for years. Everything has its own productive life and that was also true of this sweeper. It had been so reliable she decided she wanted another like it. You always knew it was well built because it weighed enough to strain your back when you used it. But because she had such good luck with it, we went to a store to purchase a new one. The store we went to carried many different brands, including: Kirby, Tyson, Bissell. Hoover, etc. The salesman asked if he could show us some of his new models too, because they had many exciting features not available in the past. When we left the store we owned a different brand than what we entered to buy. The one he sold us was considerably lighter, had more allergen filters, and was a little more affordable. We've had the new brand for several years and have been quite pleased.

At our ages, my wife and I take a few vitamin supplements. We have told the expert at the vitamin store what we were looking for, and he showed us a couple options. He explained the differences, why the prices were different, and let us choose the one we wanted. We've always been pleased with the knowledge he possesses and the time he takes to get us into a satisfactory product.

As a financial planner who also sells life insurance, I often hear a client say he is planning on buying term insurance and investing the difference in the two premiums in stocks or mutual funds. Since I offered all types of investment products I could quickly state, "If that is what you want I can provide that. However, if you will permit me a couple of minutes I can show you how you can accomplish the same thing but with some extra tax advantages." Then I would show how the universal life policy or a variable universal life insurance policy is wrapped around an annual renewable term insurance policy and the remaining premium is invested inside the policy, which is a tax-deferred device.

Every time I prepare a financial plan for clients, it is based on the objectives they have. But, there are many ways to get to the goal. It's like taking a trip from Kansas City to Denver. You can fly, you can take a bus, or you can drive and take a variety of routes to get there. You are not locked in to a specific type of travel to reach your goal. To reach financial goals you can also chose a variety of investment options depending on your risk tolerance. After considering the options available to you, you chose the one you prefer.

When I sit down with a client to present solutions, I repeat the goals the client has. Then I offer a few options (e.g., maybe Plan A, Plan B, and Plan C). I detail the pros and cons of each option and then let the client chose the one that fits his/her risk tolerance level. I don't have to pressure the client. Either option I present is designed for him/her/them to meet the specified financial goals. I also assure him/her/them that we will monitor the success of the chosen plan periodically to make future changes as they were needed. Financial products are complicated for most people, even to those who sell them, so clearly explaining the differing aspects of the products one offers can be very valuable to a client.

By now, you should be getting the picture. Sometimes if you show your customer a different option, it will lead to success. You need to do it properly, though. It has to be the right solution to form a long-term relationship with the client. Don't offer a product in place of another simply because it pays more commission. (I've faced this temptation myself.) You might make that sale, but you might not ever make another to that customer. Make sure the customer's needs come first. If you build a strong relationship by treating your client the way you would want to be treated, they'll probably bring you future business and, more importantly, they will probably recommend you to their friends.

THE PERFECT QUESTION

Before any problem can be resolved, an understanding about that problem is needed. This requires some investigative work. Information must be gathered that exposes the problem. Some types of problems are discovered through visual observation. For example, stains on your ceiling are probably a fairly good indication of a roof that is beginning to leak. A clanging noise heard from under the hood of your car most likely indicates a mechanical problem.

Most problems that cannot be ascertained by use of our senses require us to gather useful information by asking questions. For example, if a child is crying and you want to help, you need to ask the child, "What's wrong?" If you are a doctor and you want to help your patient, you need to begin your diagnosis process by asking about your patient's pain. To sell someone a new car, the car dealer needs to know what kind of car the customer wants and how it is to be used. And, to keep an employee happy, or help him or her with a problem, you need details acquired from the questioning process. In the realm of financial planning, relevant facts must be gathered if you are to help your client with his or her problem.

No progress toward any financial solution is made until a dialogue is opened with your client or prospect. You must ask questions. You must have input. Financial planners who perfect the process of gathering data through questions have greater probability of success. In fact, financial planners and sales reps often tell me that learning which questions to ask a specific client is the most important element of their success.

What questions should one ask? If the client's answers are incomplete, how can one expand their answers? Are there simple techniques that can be used to get an informative dialogue going? Let's explore methods that can help get more facts. Even though you may have heard me humorously refer to the fact-finding process as a facts-inating (pun intended) element of our business, I cannot stress enough how important this step is.

You can certainly purchase sales books that go into detail about the kinds of questions you can ask your clients, and I heartily suggest that you do. One easy way to find them is to search online. Many of these books even provide sample questions for you to ask your prospects. If you prefer to scan a book before buying it, look for these books at your local bookstore or library. Studying these books will help you enhance your fact finding process. The principles you learn from them will also be applicable in both your personal and business life.

For more than four decades I have worked with sales

representatives to help them with actual sales endeavors, or to teach them techniques that can be used to serve their clients. One thing I have discovered working with clients is that they all ask similar questions during similar presentations. They seek the same information to make a decision regarding a product. If you've been in sales for any length of time you've undoubtedly noticed this, too. If you haven't already noticed it, you'll discover that the same types of questions usually happen at approximately the same spot in each presentation. Let's look at an example to illustrate this fact.

A sales representative named David called me about his client. He had sold this client many investment products and insurance products. The two of them had a great business relationship and were friends, as well. They frequently played golf together. This client's CPA told him that his business needed a profit-sharing plan. The small business was so successful that it was time to seek more tax deductions. The CPA liked the fact that a tax deduction could be obtained while being used to accumulate a retirement account. Moreover, a qualified retirement plan usually built employee morale and encouraged employees to stay with the business.

David had never sold any type of qualified plan before. He did not know how complicated these plans were but felt he needed to try to help his client with this request. He was afraid that if he told his client he didn't offer profit sharing arrangements, the client would talk to another advisor. If some other sales rep ended up helping his client it might place David's business with the client at risk.

His client's business was a small company (less than ten

employees), and I suggested David get a copy of the employee census so I could create a proposal. To create the profit sharing proposal the census needed to show: employee names, their birthdays, their salaries, etc. After acquiring the census data, David faxed the information to me. He had obtained the information I needed within two hours. Such a prompt response showed me that his relationship with his client was pretty strong.

From the data provided, I produced a sample profit sharing illustration. My proposal showed: the contribution amount each employee would receive, a projection of the retirement benefits for the owner and each employee, and an analysis of the approximate tax savings the business would experience. I sent the package of materials by overnight carrier to David. He received it the next day. The reason I rushed my response to David was because his client was in a hurry to start the plan. He wanted to begin making deposits immediately so he would not incur a burden to contribute all of the money at the end of the year. After David received the profit sharing proposal he called. "What do I do with this proposal now?" he asked. "Remember, Steve, I've never sold a profit-sharing plan before."

There were many times that I helped sales reps make this type of presentation by doing it for the rep. This was accomplished by having the sales rep put me on a speaker phone with the rep and the client. Everyone would have an individual copy of the proposal and would follow along as I explained the numbers. Unfortunately, this time I could not use this procedure because I was going to be out of town when David and the client had their meeting. I told David that I would take time to train him on what to say as he went through the proposal. I encouraged him to ask questions and to take copious notes. I further assured him that after we went through the materials, he would be adequately prepared to make the presentation himself. Nervously, he asked, "What if the client asks me a question I don't know the answer to?"

I responded, "Then, David, just tell him you'll call him with the answer the next day. I've done enough of these over the years that I suspect we'll cover most of the questions the client will ask in our training session. Now, David, go make a photocopy of the presentation materials and call me back. That way you'll be able to make notes in the margins of your copy and study them before your presentation. You'll keep the clean version for the client."

David made the photocopies and called back. It took about an hour to go through the proposal. I told him that he would lay the proposal in front of the client and begin. I went through each section explaining it slowly enough so he could take copious notes. When questions came up, I answered them. At certain points in the proposal I would pause and tell him that near that point the client is going to ask him a question. I explained what the client would want to know and what the client would ask. Then I added, "Here's how you will answer that question." I continued explaining the proposal. I could tell David was taking notes because he would ask me to pause for a second. I showed him where each question would occur and what the question would be. He wrote my answers down so he could memorize them later.

When we were finished going over the proposal, I told David that he was ready to make the presentation. I wished him luck and said goodbye. He knew that I would not be available the day he was making the presentation, but he forged ahead because he did not want a competitor to enter his client's life.

The day after David made his presentation, I returned to my office. I picked up my phone to retrieve my messages and was greeted by a message from David. He was frantic. He wanted help RIGHT NOW! He had made the presentation on the prior day and almost yelled that he needed help as soon as possible. I lifted my phone and gave him a call.

"What's wrong, David?" I asked.

He was so excited he could barely speak. With a calm voice, I suggested he take a deep breath before continuing. He blurted, "Steve, you won't believe how the sales presentation went. I was going through the presentation and at the point where you said he would ask a question, he did. In fact, he asked the exact question you said he would!"

"And what did you do?" I asked.

"I gave him the answer you said I should. This went on throughout the presentation. He asked the questions you said he would at the points you said he would, and I gave him the answers you had provided."

"So, what's the problem, David? You seem to be wound pretty tight, even though it sounds like the presentation went really well. It sounds like you did exactly what you were supposed to."

He exhaled before answering. "Steve, it went extremely well! In fact, my client said he wanted to install the plan immediately. I hadn't discussed that option with you. I didn't know what to say."

"You must have told him something. He's been a client and friend of yours for a long time. What did you say?" I inquired.

He answered, "I didn't know what to tell him, so I just said I would bring back papers for him to sign to establish the plan."

I could tell that it was time to build David's confidence. "You did exactly the right thing, David. Now, let's talk about how to complete the profit-sharing documents." I explained how the documents should be completed. He took the documents back to the client to be signed. The client was happy. The CPA was happy. And, David was extremely happy. Because of David's learning experience with this case, he felt he could approach other clients about retirement plans for their businesses. He began contacting his client base to show the advantages of tax-favored retirement plans to them.

Throughout my career I have discovered that sales representatives often display similar traits as their clients. Most reps ask me the same types of questions that other reps do during our phone calls or meetings. The most common question I hear is: "I've read a lot of books about questions that I should ask clients when I meet with them, but there are so many questions to ask that I don't know which ones to use. I'm sure that different ones should be used when selling different types of products or service, but I don't know which ones to use."

You need to know that I'm no different from most sales reps. I've just been around longer, and I've met with a few more clients. Therefore, I have been able to learn what works with my clients. But, when I was a newbie, I faced the same dilemmas when I sat down to gather facts with my client. I, too, wanted to know how to get a dialogue going. I needed to know how to get the prospect or client to open up and tell me what he/she really needed or wanted. Eventually, I discovered how to use "The Perfect Question." This is a question I developed from my own experiences.

I call the question "The Perfect Question" because I use the word "perfect" in it. It's actually a pretty simple question, but it reveals a lot of information. After I ask the question, I just need to wait for the client to answer. Then, I need to take notes as fast as I can. And, it doesn't matter what the topic is. All I need to do is alter the question slightly to fit the need we are addressing.

The basic format of the question is this: "Mr./Ms. Client, for a couple of minutes I'm going to ask you to forget what your CPA has told you. Forget what you've read on this topic in industry magazines. And, definitely forget what your know-it-all brother-in-law has told you about this subject. Mr./Ms. Prospect, if I could design the perfect _____ (fill in the blank), what would it look like?" You can insert the appropriate word or words to fit the sales situation into the blank. For example, if I could design the perfect "retirement plan" for you, what would it look like? Or, perhaps, if I could design the perfect "financial plan" for you, what would it look like? Or, maybe, if I could provide the perfect "disability plan" for you, what would it look like?

The "perfect" part of the question works in scenarios other than selling. "Mr./Ms. Boss, you've given me this project to work on. If I produce the perfect result for you, what will that look like?" "Honey, if we went looking for the "perfect" house, what, in your mind, will it need to have?" You get the picture. Ask the question, then, remember what the answer was. Take good notes or record the answer.

The most important thing the perfect question reveals is what the responder wants. After you know what is desired you can design a solution that fits the "want." If you can provide a solution that fits what is wanted, the responder will be happier. Your prospect will be more likely to do business with you.

Begin using the perfect question in your business and personal life. You will find that the question will open communication lines with everyone. You'll get a lot more information using this broad question than if you use questions designed to garner a specific fact. Most answers will contain several sentences. You will need to learn to write fast, or you will need to ask the other person to slow down. In those cases when your client will let you tape the interview you will find that to be helpful, but I have found that many people become less talkative when the recorder is turned on.

If you are trying to make a sale, this perfect question reveals the client's "hot" button. Answers to the question tell you want the prospect really wants. The prospect tells you what is important to him or her. In other words you learn about the psychology behind the client's desire. This is important because it's the psychology that helps you make the sale. Numbers alone rarely make a sale for you.

Few car buyers decide to purchase a car solely because it gets good gas mileage. They buy the car because of the way it makes them feel. They "love" the color. It feels right when they sit in it.

My wife doesn't buy a dress because the size number is what she wants. (However, if the dress is a size that is erroneously labeled four sizes smaller than it really is, she might be tempted). She buys the dress because of the way she feels when she looks in the mirror. The color flatters her. It makes her look thin. It is sexy. I know you can all relate to these thoughts.

When you know what is important to your prospect, you will be in a better position to recommend a more appropriate and suitable solution. Better solutions foster long-term relationships with clients. Also, the closer your solutions are to what the client wants, the better your closing ratio will be.

So, if I could write the perfect story for you to read, what would it be?

IS THERE A PROSPECT SITTING
UNDER YOUR NOSE?

We human beings are quick to make judgements based on our senses. We might determine a steak to be fresh based on how red it is, and it might simply be red because of the dye used to color it. If we hear a clanking sound under the hood of our car we might assume that there is something wrong with the motor, when it might just be a loose piece of metal tapping against the inside of the engine compartment. When a dog growls at us we believe it is dangerous, but if it is like my dog, it is simply indicating that it wants to play.

We do the same thing with other humans. If they dress shabbily we assume they are poor. If they drive an expensive car, we guess them to be rich. We might assume that the person wearing a cross is religious, but maybe he or she just likes it as a piece of jewelry. Perhaps they are covered in tattoos so we think they are dangerous. We classify people based on our frames of reference. We, as financial planners, often do the same thing with potential prospects.

When I was a youngster, there was a man in the region who pumped out septic tanks. He was a nice man and worked hard. He did a job most of us wouldn't want to do. Behind his back, people referred to him as the "honey dipper." Sometimes he called himself this, too. Often, it was said as a joke, but it still had derogatory tones to it. He did not wear fancy attire. He did not drive an expensive car – his cars were usually several years old. His children wore hand-me-downs. People assumed the family was poor. When he died, he left an estate of over $2,000,000. This was around forty years ago when $2,000,000 seemed like a lot of money.

A few years ago I worked with a financial planner who had a client that owned a salvage yard (sometimes we call them junkyards). He salvaged parts from cars and sold them, or he used parts to rebuild cars and then sold those. He lived in an unassuming three-bedroom house, drove a used truck that he had built from parts in his junkyard, and was usually seen wearing dirty jeans around town. He, too, was a very nice man, but employed frugality in his everyday life. My financial planning friend helped service the pension plan that had been set up for the salvage business. He met with the business owner many times and never assumed the owner had a lot of money. When the junkyard owner died, his family found over one million dollars cash in the furnace vents of his three-bedroom house. This, too, was back when $1,000,000 was considered a sizeable amount of money.

As a financial planner, I also have made assumptions about people. Sometimes my assumptions cost me a business relationship. Depending on where a prospect lived, or what their occupations were, I would judge if they were a viable prospect. Many times, I found out later that I had erred in my judgement. Because I never approached them, they did business with someone else. Sometimes the purchases they made were large. Even for those cases that were small, doing business with them would have taken little time and the associated expenses would have been low.

One example involves a wholesaler that had its office next to ours. In fact, it took us about seven seconds to walk from our office door to theirs. We would visit almost every morning. We shared cups of coffee, discussed news events, sports teams, family accomplishments, and the like. However, we did not discuss business. They were not even sure what we did. The name on our office just listed the partners. It did not indicate what services we provided.

One day while I was on the phone one of the wholesalers came into the office to get a cup of coffee while waiting for their coffee maker to brew a new batch. She waited for my call to end so she could bid me a good morning. As she waited she heard me discussing the funding of a Simplified Employee Pension Plan (SEP, for short) with the client. When I finished, she said, "Do you guys set up SEPs?"

"We do," I said, "It is part of many financial services we offer."

She gave a small sigh. "I sure wish we had known that. We would have gladly done business with your firm since we know you so well, but we didn't know you offered those types of plans. We set up a SEP using someone else." Our financial services firm was so busy chasing after large cases that we totally ignored a simple sale about ten feet away from our office. We probably would not have made a lot of money selling them a SEP but it would have been a simple transaction. Moreover, they were a wholesaler. They had many clients. They might have opened doors to some of their clients so we could help their clients with their financial concerns. It would have been so easy for us to let them know what services we offered. But, we didn't. We made a judgement that they would not be a viable candidate for our services. We were wrong.

Another case involved a part-time assistant that we hired through Kelly Services. Because our business was under pressure to generate high revenues, many full-time assistants did not stay long. In the interim looking for a new assistant, we would hire a "Kelly Girl" to help (today we know better than to call them "girls" because a lot of the employees are male). We paid the Kelly organization around $11.00 per hour for the part-time employee and Kelly paid his or her salary directly to the assistant.

One day, after one of the Kelly assistants had worked for us for two and a half days, she approached me. She asked, "What, exactly, does your company do? Do you guys help people manage their money?"

I explained how we, as financial planners, helped our clients accumulate and protect their assets. I was curious why she had asked her question. Was she interested in a full-time position with us? Did she want to begin an investment program? Did she know someone who needed our services?

Here was a young lady (about 28 years old) who was asking us about how we helped people with money problems. I had to satisfy my curiosity. "Jill, I'm curious why you want to know about how we help people with money. Do you have some money that needs to be invested or managed?" I was pretty sure she didn't because she was getting about $7.00 per hour after Kelly took its cut.

"I don't have any money, but I know someone who does," she said.

"Do they have a significant amount?" I asked.

"She doesn't have a lot today, but she is getting a lot in a couple of weeks," she stated.

"Would you be willing to share who the person is and how much money she is getting?" I paused to see if she would answer.

She did not even hesitate. "It's my mom and she is getting $6,000,000 in a couple of weeks." I was stunned by her answer. Who would have connected this young lady to $6,000,000? Today that is a lot of money. Back then, it was an enormous amount.

"How is she coming into $6,000,000? Is this an inheritance?" Here was a potential prospect sitting under our noses, and we had been ignoring her. In fact, we were probably not treating her very well, at all. All we did was issue commands to her, and we didn't always do it with a smile. I suspected that our approach would change once all the partners knew her mother's circumstances. I needed more information, so I waited for her answer.

"The money is coming from a settlement of a lawsuit. About six years ago, my father was driving through Texas and was hit by an oil hauler. He was killed. The driver of the oil truck was clearly at fault. We were advised by our attorney to bring suit, so we did. We have finally been through all of the appeals process, and the oil company has been directed by the court to pay a large sum to my mom. After the attorneys get their share, she will get around $6,000,000. She's never had that kind of money so she is going to need help managing it."

"Are you sure there will not be any more delays?" I asked.

"There are no more appeals that can be used to delay payment. The oil company will be paying the money out. My mom has already completed the necessary paperwork to receive the money," she replied.

I leaned back in my chair. "If your mom has been involved in court battles this long, and she knows the money will soon be paid, she has undoubtedly contacted some financial planners. Am I correct in that assumption?"

"She has, but it has been a difficult challenge for her. She doesn't know who to trust. She called three different financial planners and likes two of them. However, she doesn't know if they are any good. She doesn't know if they produce good returns. She doesn't know if they have her interests at the forefront. Can you help us in any way?"

At this point I knew that we were not operating from a position of strength. Jill's mom had already had discussions with two other financial planners. They had already had many conversations. While their relationship was limited she already had one with them. She didn't have one with us. We had not talked to her at all. I tried to ease Jill's concerns. "We would be glad to help your mother, Jill. That's what we do here. We help people deal with financial issues. I don't know who your mom has been talking to, but I have an idea that she might want to consider."

"I appreciate your help. What's your idea?" she asked.

"Jill, you and your mom don't know any of us, but she really doesn't know the other planners either. So, I'm going to suggest that she take a cautious approach with her money. My suggestion is that she put $2,000,000 with each of the planners. That helps protect a large portion of her money if one of the planners is not very talented. Then, after two or three years she will know which one she prefers. Who knows, she might like having three different money managers to compete for her business, and she might decide to maintain the three relationships for years to come."

Jill responded, "We had not considered using more than one planner. I think that is a great idea. That helps protect her money if one of the managers is not very good. I'll talk to her about this approach tonight." After she left for the day, I told the partners about my conversation with Jill. They were surprised. They liked the approach I used. The next day they began treating Jill differently. Jill's mom took my advice. She split the money between different managers.

Sometimes a prospect is camouflaged a little too well to be quickly recognizable. Such was the case with this next example.

Doug was an insurance agent who worked numerous estate planning cases. Many considered him to be an expert in this field. One day, he called me to discuss his latest case. He was baffled by his prospect's statements. The prospect was the president of a corporation that was worth around $10 million dollars. He was mid-fifties, single, and had three children (two daughters, and a son). The son worked with dad (the prospect) in the business. The daughters had no interest in the business. Doug knew there was some type of estate planning issue at play, but every time he broached the subject with the prospect, the prospect told him he did not have an estate tax problem. "How can this be?" Doug asked.

"Doug, there are ways people can avoid estate taxes. One example is to leave all of their property to a charity. That yields a complete write-off of the assets against the estate. Without any ownership of assets there is no property to tax and no estate taxes will occur. I doubt that your prospect has traveled this road, though –not with three children he probably wants to leave something to. My first inclination is to find out if your prospect owns the corporate stock. That could be what he is trying to say. If he doesn't own any stock, the value of the corporation will not be included in his estate. Only property one owns is included for tax purposes. You need to ask him if he owns the business. After you have the answer, call me back and we'll discuss the case."

A couple of days later Doug called to discuss the case. "You were right about ownership of the corporation," he said. "This prospect doesn't own one share of the business. Shortly after he began his business he could tell it would be very successful so he created an irrevocable trust and gifted the stock into it. The trust hires him to manage the company, but he has no control over the trust assets. Since he doesn't own any of the corporation none of its value will be included in his taxable estate. I guess he was right. He doesn't have any estate tax problem, so there is not a sales opportunity here."

"Wait a second, Doug," I said. "I think you may be missing the real problem." I think there is a problem here that needs to be addressed. And, you should be in a good situation to help solve the problem."

I could tell he did not really believe me. "What problem do you see?"

"Doug, from what you've told me, I think there is a problem that will eventually involve the children. Eventually, they are going to inherit the business through the trust. Maybe the trust is authorized to distribute shares to the children. Maybe it will hold the shares for the children. At any rate, I think the business will eventually cause conflict between the children. The daughters will only be interested in the business for the income it will produce. The son will think he deserves a larger share because he will be running the operation. If the daughters have authority to vote their shares in the trust, they might oust their brother from corporate management. There is a huge potential for conflict in this family. Yet, there are ways to avoid these conflicts."

I continued. "Doug, I know you have heard of a buy-sell agreement. You've even set them up before. This agreement usually specifies that certain surviving owners of a business will buy out the shares of the deceased owner. This prevents a surviving partner from being in business with heirs whose only interest in the business is how much income it can generate for them. The agreement requires a surviving partner to buy out the heir's shares, and it obligates the heirs to sell the deceased's shares to the surviving business owner. To assure that the surviving business owner has the money needed to make the purchase, life insurance is often purchased on each owner. Even though this corporation's shares are owned by a trust, a buy-sell agreement can still be used. The trust can purchase life insurance on the father. When the father dies, the trust receives the life insurance proceeds and uses those proceeds to buy out the shares left to the daughters. When the transaction is completed, the daughters will have cash and the son will have the business. You should bring up this subject with the father and his children."

Doug mentioned the coming dilemma to the parties involved. They could already see the looming problem. They met with the attorneys to draft the buy-sell agreement owned by the trust. Life insurance was purchased and owned by the trust. The trust was the beneficiary of the policies. In this case, Doug had been approaching the prospect with the wrong topic. After the buy-sell arrangement was completed, Doug was in a position to talk to each of the children about his or her future estate issues. After all, each was to receive a large sum when their father died. Sometimes you just need to start at the right place to see where the real prospect is. In this case, it was the children, not the father.

I worked with another financial planner making presentations to the employees of a multi-state employer. The employer worried about its employees. It wanted them to have help with their personal estate planning and retirement planning concerns. We were even allowed to address the employees at the various corporate work sites during work hours. The planner I was working with made presentations regarding estate issues (e.g., wills, guardianships, trusts, taxes, etc.). I made presentations about accumulating retirement assets. After we finished people filled out a card to request our follow up if they wanted help. Following completion of one of our sessions a young female attendee approached.

"I listened to you discuss estate planning issues. Do you think you could help my family?" she asked.

"Do you own property?" She didn't look like someone that had many assets. She did not seem to be a viable prospect for our services. (Never judge a book by its cover).

"Oh, no!" she said. "I don't own anything today. I only make $8.00 per hour, so I cannot accumulate much money."

Again, I was curious why she was asking this question. "Are you planning on having assets someday?"

"I expect that I may inherit some property someday," she said. "Maybe you could visit with my father about his estate planning needs. I'm sure if I suggested that he talk to you, he would."

"If you think he has a fair amount of assets, we would be happy to help," I said. I was thinking that this was probably going to be a waste of our time but since the employer had offered us this opportunity, I decided to be polite.

She added, "He says he has significant assets. He has some pretty successful oil wells."

Now she had my attention. "Has he ever indicated what his total assets are?" I asked.

"He has," she replied. "He said his property has been valued at $30 million."

Calmly, I answered. "If you want to arrange a visit with us, we will be happy to see if we can provide beneficial services to him. He probably already has an estate planning team, but sometimes we recognize something that still needs to be addressed. How would you like to approach this with your father?"

It's easy to overlook a prospect. Sometimes we make assumptions that are incorrect. Maybe the reason we don't recognize the prospect is that our knowledge base doesn't contain the information needed to recognize that a problem exists. I remember that as I studied for my CLU and CFP designations, I was often amazed that shortly after I studied a topic I would run into a prospect with a problem I had just learned about. The problem had undoubtedly always existed, but I did not recognize it because my knowledge base did not possess the information I needed. If there is one important piece of advice you can garner from me, it's that you need to continue to study. Regardless of your profession, the more you learn, the more efficient you will be. As you learn more, you'll recognize issues that need to be addressed. Often, you'll also learn the manner in which these issues ought to be addressed.

Every organization has marketing professionals. People need to know that a business exists and what products and benefits it provides before they will patronize it. Many marketing professionals in a company have been in sales positions themselves. Their experience helps them to recognize a viable prospect. If you are not sure if you are looking at a viable prospect, call one of your company's marketing professionals to discuss your case. Perhaps the professional will recognize the need that is currently hidden from you. You might be going down the wrong path. You might not see the problem the prospect needs to address. You might not know how to broach the topic with your client or prospect. A good relationship with a knowledgeable marketing professional can greatly enhance your success.

The other point I want to make is that you need to let people you have contact with know what you do. And, don't make assumptions about an acquaintance's needs. To recognize a need, you have to gather information. What assets does the prospect have? What are the prospect's goals? Are you able to provide the services your client needs, or should you seek help from someone with more expertise to assist you in developing solutions for your client?

Just like my case with the Kelly employee, you could be looking at a large case that looks small on the surface. Or, like in Doug's case you might be trying to fit a square peg into a round hole. Get help if you need to. Don't overlook the prospect sitting right under your nose.

YOU AIN'T DONE YET

Aaron was a successful financial services representative. He had been serving clients for several years. His income was above average. Clients respected him, and he had learned to depend on help from his mentors. When he encountered a situation creating a challenge, he had no reservations about calling mentors for help.

Aaron had just been contacted by a prospect that was getting laid off from the only company he had ever worked for. The prospect was 56 years old and had $3,000,000 in his 401(k) plan account. The client, Phil, talked about rolling his 401(k) account to an IRA. Aaron was happy to help and wanted to make sure the rollover was the best strategy for Phil. Aaron called me to discuss the case.

"What facts do you have about the case?" I asked.

Aaron answered, "The client works in a computer-related industry. He has been there since he graduated from college. He has held an officer position for several years and earned a very good income. It looks like the company thinks he can be replaced with a younger geek at a much lower income. That's often how it is in computer-related companies."

"What can you tell me about his 401(k) account? What's the makeup of the assets?"

"Phil's 401(k) account has around $3,000,000. $1,000,000 of the account is in his employer's stock. The other $2,000,000 is in an assortment of mutual funds. He is fairly well diversified. He has had good growth during his participation in the plan."

"Aaron, do you know when the employer stock was purchased?"

"The prospect said that the shares were purchased in the first five years that he worked for the company. The retirement plan was a profit-sharing plan back then. It became a 401(k) plan several years later. The company was purchased by another company (the current owner) about five or six years after he started working there. To purchase the company, a stock swap occurred. The buying company's stock was traded for the old company's stock. Everyone was happy with this type of purchase. Phil said that if an existing shareholder accepted the new stock for his old shares, no taxable event occurred at that time. Taxation would only happen when the new stock shares were eventually sold. New shares were also swapped for any shares that were in the profit-sharing plan, too, but that would have been a non-taxable transaction anyway because the shares were owned by the trustee of a qualified plan."

"Aaron, you've done a great job of fact-finding. That's exactly how many corporations buy other corporations. It's called a like-kind exchange. The tax laws allow the exchange to occur without causing a taxable event at that time. Without a tax law like this, many owners would be reluctant to sell. Did you ask your prospect how much the stock was worth when it was originally purchased by the profit-sharing plan? Profit-sharing plans are required to track this amount. The amount paid for the stock is called its "cost basis."

Aaron replied, "I didn't ask him about the price paid for the stock. Is that important?"

"It could be, I said, but, let's see what your prospect says."

"Okay," responded Aaron. "I'll call him right now."

A couple of hours later Aaron called me. He had been able to reach his prospect and ask him about the cost basis of the stock. His prospect told him he did not know the answer, but he would find out and call Aaron back in a couple of days.

"Aaron, this is a significant piece of information. Depending on the answer Phil provides in a couple of days it could give you a lot of leverage with this prospect."

"How does this give me more leverage? He asked.

"Aaron, is this a prospect you called on, or did he call you?"

"He called me. I had never met him before."

"This is a 56-year-old man who is about to lose his job. Most people in that situation are a little nervous. If they cannot find a comparable job, they've got to make their retirement account last the rest of their lives. Because of his concerns about making his money last, I suspect that you are not the only financial planner he called. It would not surprise me if he called four or five others. He wants to make sure his investment performs the way he needs it to so he can maintain a desired lifestyle. Did he tell you what he plans to do?"

I could hear Aaron flipping pages of his notes. "I asked him if he planned to try to get another job. He told me that he was too young to retire, but he wasn't going to work for someone else. He said that a job with another employer could be eliminated just as easily as his current job had. So, what he really plans to do is buy a business. He's already found one he likes. It's a small business with good revenues. He said he needed to use $900,000 from his 401(k) to buy it."

"Again, Aaron, you've done excellent fact-finding. Let's see what answer he comes up with regarding the cost basis of the stock. Based on what you've told me so far I think you will be in a good position to get this rollover. I think we can propose a solution that will be tax efficient, accomplish exactly what he wants, and you will be the only financial planner that provides this solution. You will be more popular than the other financial planners he called. You will be the only one that has provided the solution he needs."

"Why do you say that?" asked Aaron.

"Because if someone had already presented the solution we are going to show him, he would already know the cost basis amount paid by the purchasing company for the stock."

A couple of days later Aaron called. "I've got the cost basis for the stock. It was purchased so many years ago that the cost basis is really low."

"What's the amount?" I asked.

"The cost basis amount for the stock is $64,000, but it is worth around $1,000,000 today."

"That's fairly common in the technology field. Look at what Microsoft cost 40 years ago. Today, those who bought shares back then for a few thousand dollars and held them are multimillionaires."

"So, what's this great idea we are going to show him?"

"It's about the 'net unrealized appreciation' of the stock. In fact, that's the term used by the tax code. The appreciation (gain) in the price of the stock has not been taxed. In other words the gain has not been realized. In this case, the stock cost $64,000 when it was purchased by the plan. Today, it is worth $1,000,000. There is a gain of $936,000 that has not been reported, or 'realized.' When a qualified plan participant is eligible to take a distribution (e.g., retirement, disability, etc.), the tax code allows the participant to take his stock as a distribution of shares instead of taking cash. When the stock is distributed, or transferred, to the participant the cost basis amount becomes reportable as ordinary income – in this case $64,000 would need to be reported. Once ownership of the stock is complete the shareholder can sell the stock. The $936,000 of net unrealized appreciation when the stock is sold later, even if only a day or two later, is taxed as a capital gain. And, what's the maximum tax rate for capital gains?"

"Right now it's twenty percent,"

"That right, Aaron. So, Phil can take the employer stock instead of cash and report $64,000 as ordinary income. $936,000 of unrealized gain on the stock will be a capital gain taxed at 20%. For now, we'll ignore state income taxes for illustration purposes. After taxes, Phil will have a fairly large portion of the $1,000,000 he needs to buy the business he desires. Phil probably has enough other personal assets to make up any difference needed to reach the $900,000 price for his new business. After all, he was a corporate officer for several years. Aaron, you won't get a $3,000,000 rollover because he'll use the proceeds from the stock to purchase the new business. But, you will almost certainly get a rollover of the other $2,000,000. I'll send you some information about the 'net unrealized appreciation' tax advantage for him to take to his accountant." (I sent pages from the tax code explaining how the net unrealized appreciation rule works. Most CPAs and other tax preparers do not encounter this situation so they are unaware of this break.)

A little over a week went by and Aaron called. "Steve, I want to thank you for your help on this rollover. The material you sent got the prospect's accountant excited. He did not know about this tax rule. After he read it, he told my prospect that this was what he needed to do. We completed the paperwork for the rollover last week. I really appreciate what you did. After I presented this solution to Phil, no other financial planner was even considered for the rollover."

"Aaron, I'm really happy that you were able to help this client achieve his objectives. Back where I grew up, when a project was not completed people would tell me, 'you ain't done yet.' And that's what I'm telling you right now. You ain't done yet." I also joked that where I grew up it was common to hear people say "bidness", instead of business. He laughed.

"Oh," he said. "I see what you are saying. The money hasn't transferred to the rollover account so I might need to follow up to make sure everything goes as planned."

"Well, Aaron," I said, "You do need to make sure the rollover goes through properly, but that's not what I meant. There are more issues here that must be addressed with this client."

"What do you mean, Steve? What other issues do I need to discuss with my new client?"

"Aaron, this client was an officer in his company for several years. He had $3,000,000 in his 401(k) plan. It is rare to find people who have $3,000,000 in their 401(k) accounts. But, one thing I have noticed in my work as a financial planner is that people who have $3,000,000 in their qualified plan usually have other assets, too. Phil probably has an expensive house. Maybe he had a deferred compensation plan in addition to his 401(k). He's 56 years old, so he might have some inherited property. His wife might have some, too."

I continued. "I think you need to find out how much this client actually has. He may have estate planning issues. He might not have an estate large enough to incur federal estate taxes, but he probably wants to make sure his property takes care of his heirs. He wants it to get to the proper people. Since he's buying a business, he might want to leave the business to one child, but provide equal cash value to another child. A life insurance policy could be used to equalize the inheritances. Even though he might not have a federal estate tax impact there might be a fairly large state inheritance tax his heirs will experience. You should broach this topic with him."

"Okay, Steve. Right now he is happy with the solution we provided for his 401(k) money. I'll tell him we need to discuss estate planning with his attorney. I don't know why he would listen to me, though."

"Aaron, you're the one guy in town he will listen to. You brought him the perfect solution he needed for his 401(k) money when no one else did. If there is anyone he'll listen to, it's you."

"Okay. I'll bring up estate planning with him and see where it goes."

A couple of weeks passed and I had not heard from Aaron, so I called to follow up on this case.

"I'm glad you called. I want to thank you again. I mentioned that he should address estate planning issues. He didn't even have a will. We had good meetings with his attorney and he is drafting trust documents right now. The attorney even recommended he purchase life insurance to cover state inheritance taxes, help to equalize distributions to heirs, and make sure his wife is adequately provided for, especially since the income from the $2,000,000 in the IRA is subject to federal and state income taxes."

"It sounds like you are taking great steps to help your client sleep at night. He'll be happy to know that his financial plan will take care of his family. But, Aaron, at this point I need to say again, you ain't done yet."

"You're right about that, Steve. It'll take a little longer to get the legal work done by the attorney. Also, the life insurance policy is currently in the underwriting department so it might be a couple of months before the policy is issued."

"I'm glad you're moving ahead on this but there are still many issues that need to be addressed with this client. Let's look at a few:

- We know that your client purchased a business. Did he buy it and will he be the sole owner? If so, will he want to leave the business to an heir but give cash to other heirs? Did he borrow any money in addition to his $900,000, and if so, how does the loan get paid off if something happens to him?

- Did he simply buy a portion of the business and is now part owner with other partners? If so, what happens to a partner's share when one of them dies or becomes disabled? A business continuation agreement may be needed to make sure the surviving partner does not end up owning the business with demanding heirs.

- Are there employee benefits in the business he purchased? Should these be reviewed? Perhaps there are cheaper or better plans that could be implemented.

- Is there a retirement plan in his business? If there is one thing this man knows it's the value of a qualified plan. After all, his 401(k) plan helped him purchase the business or a share in it.

"I think you get the idea now, Aaron. You may be able to help this client in many new ways. You may be able to save him money on benefits he provides to employees. You may be able to help him accumulate more retirement assets. It's worth a discussion with him about these things. He may not be ready to address them now, but you can plant the seed for addressing them in the future."

Aaron's case is similar to cases we all experience. After making a sale, we are very happy that we made the sale and helped our client solve a problem. But, too often, we don't dig deep enough to recognize that other issues exist for the client.

Even a clothing sales person will ask you if you need a tie to match the shirt or suit you just bought. If you just bought a new dress with a repeating red line running through it every three inches, a diligent sales rep might ask you if you need a pair of shoes the same red color to enhance the outfit.

If you are not sure what issues should be addressed, ask your prospect. You might say, "Mr./Ms. Prospect, we worked hard to find a solution for your problem and we were successful in finding one. But now I want to make sure we address any other concerns you have. Is there some other issue we should look at? Even if you are not ready to work on it today, we can put it on the table for follow up later." Then wait to see what he or she says. I've often been surprised by what my prospects said. Many of them had concerns about other pressing issues and without their input those concerns would have been ignored.

You need to make sure that you understand what I'm saying. This is NOT about just trying to sell something else to your client. We don't want to force a prospect to purchase something he or she doesn't want. That might damage a long term relationship and cost us future business with the prospect. Your goal is to help your client find solutions for as many concerns as he or she has. If you haven't done that, you ain't done yet!

LACY'S STORY

Because I hold various financial services designations (see cover), I am frequently called upon to review sales materials for accuracy. This was especially true when I worked in corporate offices. I would review materials to double check cost-of-living adjustments, tax rules, calculations, sales viability, PowerPoint presentation accuracy, etc. Because of the importance of the accuracy of the sales materials, these reviews usually involved several people. Nothing makes a sale more difficult for you than when a competitor can point to something that is incorrect in your company's sales brochure. Your company's credibility and yours are called into question when that happens.

Lacy worked in the marketing department of a home office and approached me to review a letter that the company was going to use in a direct mail campaign. She put it in my inbox and asked me to try to look at it in the next couple of days. I agreed and she said she could drop by later in the week.

A couple of days later, she peeked in to my office and asked,

"Steve, were you able to review my materials?"

"I was," I replied. "I added my comments and corrections to the materials. But before you leave, may we take a few minutes to discuss the letters?"

"Sure," she said. She sat down in the chair facing me and asked, "Is there a problem?"

"Lacy, the materials you provided were similar to those produced throughout our industry. They explained the product, gave relevant facts, listed a few rules, and suggested the recipient give us or one of our reps a call. I guess my concern is how effective these materials will be. After the recipient reads the brochure, will he or she actually take action? Or, will the recipient even open the letter in the first place?"

"What do you mean?" she asked.

"I'm wondering if the letters will produce adequate results for the costs associated with them. You've got the expense for the time involved in their production. Then, you've got the cost of printing the letters. After that, you've got the cost of mailing them to the selected prospects."

She responded, "We all know there are costs connected to a direct mail campaign. We also know that direct mail programs generally do not generate a lot of activity. Most of the time three people out of one-hundred send back the reply cards. But, if a sales rep gets some of the people to become clients those clients often become a source for referred leads. For some reps that are reluctant to make sales calls, direct mail can offer a way to approach new people. When the rep gets a response, he or she knows it is someone who is interested in the topic discussed. In other words, it is a 'warm' prospect."

"Lacy, I concur that direct mail letters have their place in the marketing world. All I'm saying is that care should be taken to design materials of interest to the recipient. Didn't you once tell me that your husband has his own business?"

"He does," she said. "He's been at it a long time and has a great clientele. He is known for providing quality in his construction business. His reputation helps him maintain a steady line of prospects."

I leaned back in my chair and looked at her. "Tell me this, Lacy, does he ever get direct mail letters in his business?"

She sighed. "He gets them all the time. He receives a few every day. His response to them is one of the things I find aggravating."

"Are you annoyed by the fact that he gets direct mail letters, or are you annoyed about what he does with them?"

"I'm upset about what he does with them," she said.

"What's does he do with them?" I waited to see what her answer would be.

"He pulls a trash can in front of him and begins going through the pile. More than half of the letters go directly into the trash can without ever being opened. It's really aggravating for me to watch him."

She was helping me make my point. "So, do you say anything to him when he is doing this?" I asked.

"Of course I do. I tell him he is annoying me. I tell him he is making a negative comment about my job. I tell him that I oversee the production of these types of letters every day. I remind him that I'm in charge of the company's direct mail campaigns. I sure hope the people who get the letters I developed don't treat them the same way he treats the ones he gets. But, my comments do no good. He just ignores them and keeps on tossing the letters in the trash. Sometimes, I think he does it just to upset me. He smirks at me while he is doing it. I tell him continuously that he is making fun of my job. I remind him several times as he goes through his ritual."

I'm sure I had a little grin as I responded. "Lacy, when you tell him that he is making fun of your job, you are not being accurate."

"Yes, I am," she said. "I head up the direct mail program here. It is my job to oversee the production of direct mail contacts. The success of a mailing campaign falls on me."

"Put that way, I would have to agree with you. But, your husband is throwing away his direct mail letters without even opening them. Producing direct mail letters that people never open is not your job. Your job is to produce direct mail letters that people WILL open. You need to try to increase the percentage of letters that recipients open each time a mailing is sent. Once opened, the materials need to generate enough interest for people to want more information. I realize that the materials need to satisfy the company's compliance department, so some of the sales sizzle will be gone, but the first important step is getting a prospect to open the envelope."

She was getting a little upset. I could tell because her face had a crimson glow. She stood her ground. "It sounds easy, but getting people to open direct mail is hard. People are just too busy to do it."

I thought it was time to say something positive. It was time to show I understood what she was saying. "You are right, Lacy. Today people are pulled in a lot of directions. It is hard to get them to take a couple of seconds to do almost anything. Their jobs take significant amounts of their time. Their families also require time. Also, some time needs to be devoted to recreation so they don't go crazy. And, they still need to get some restful sleep as part of their daily activities. May I tell you a short story to illustrate what I am trying to say about effective direct mail campaigns?"

I could tell that she wondered how she was going to work my story into her allotted schedule, but she remained polite. "Sure. I'd like to hear what you have to say. I am always interested in learning as much as I can."

"Lacy, this is just an example. It's a story from my life several years ago. The producers in my firm had just finished a very successful year. We were rapidly approaching a new year and wanted it to be even more successful. We decided to take actions to increase sales revenue. We knew that one way to increase sales income is by using efficient means to see more prospects. We had never tried a direct mail campaign before, but we decided it was worth trying to see what kind of results could be produced. We had heard the statistics related to direct mail campaigns and knew we wanted to experience better results. We had a meeting in early January and developed a unique plan.

"The next day I went to a local office supply store and purchased envelopes. I think they thought I was a little strange, because I bought almost every one of their pink and red envelopes. I loaded them into my car and took them back to the office. Then, we had a meeting to determine which company brochures we would use for our mailing.

"For businesses, we selected meaningful topics (e.g., employee benefits, business succession, key person coverages, and the like). For individuals, we selected brochures about retirement planning. After getting the necessary brochures from our companies (all compliance approved) we were ready to begin our mailings. We had company-approved sales materials to insert in to the envelopes.

"We had lists of addresses to which these envelopes would be sent. This was a long time ago, but we still had the capability to do a word processing mail merge to pull the addresses and put them on the envelopes. However, we chose not to do a word processing mail merge. Instead, we spent a little time every day addressing the envelopes by hand. We took our time to use the best handwriting we could. The best penmanship in our offices came from a couple of our assistants, so we had them address the envelopes for us. We did not make this choice because we wanted to delegate the task. We had them address the envelopes because the handwriting was prettier and more legible.

"I had been informed by a friend that one could get postage stamps with the word 'love' on them. I checked with the post office and found out that it was true. We could get 'love' stamps. So we did. We decided to use these stamps instead of our bulk mailing account.

When we addressed the envelopes we did not include a return address on the envelope. Only the prospect's address was displayed on the envelope. The "love" stamp was on the front in the upper right corner."

"So, we had started this process in early January. When do you think we mailed the letters?"

She pondered my question, pushed her hand through her hair, and said, "I really don't know. It seems like a lot of work for nothing to me. When did you mail the letters?"

I responded, "We mailed them on February 12th. That meant most of the recipients would get them on February 14th. What day is February 14th?"

Lacy knew this answer. "It's Valentine's Day."

"That is correct. It IS Valentine's Day. So, Lacy, if you get a hand-written, pink or red envelope with a stamp that says "love" on it on Valentine's Day, will you open it, or will you simply throw it in the trash?"

"I see where you are going with your story. I'd open it. So would everyone else who got one. If nothing else, I'd be curious who it was from. Could it be from a boyfriend? In my case, could it be from my husband or other family member? Could it be from a secret admirer? I would be afraid of upsetting the person who sent it to me by not opening it, especially if it turned out to be a close loved one. I would have to open it."

"That's the way the recipients of our letters felt. They had to open them. Virtually all of them got opened. We had business owners and individuals call us to tell us they thought it was a great marketing technique. In some cases we were able to schedule appointments. In others, the timing was wrong, or they already had an advisor they liked and did not want to change. At any rate, our goal was to have the recipients open the letters, and it worked."

"Steve, I'm not sure our compliance people will let us use this technique."

"I suspect they may not. But, you may be able to develop other successful ways to make the program more effective. If a sales rep uses this technique, I would encourage him or her to use compliance approved materials in the envelope. But, half the direct mail battle is won if the recipient of the letter opens it. If the envelope is simply tossed in the trash before it is opened, a lot of expense and work has been wasted."

"I made a few small changes to the direct mail materials you gave me to make the information correct. Now, it's your job to figure out how you can make the people who get the letters open them."

For those reading this article please note that I'm not advocating that you use this technique, although I have talked to sales reps who have used it and who have had great success. What I am suggesting to you is that you try to put yourself in your prospect's shoes, not just with direct mail pieces but with any contact you use (cold calling, telephone calls, etc.). Ask yourself, what would make me want to have further discussions with a financial advisor? What could a financial advisor say to me that would make me want to hear more? Make sure whatever you design gets the approval of your compliance department before you use it, but be creative in showing your prospects and clients how you and your company's products can help them. Maybe your results will be better than the statistics.

THE VALUE OF ONE'S WORD

My father was a man of high integrity, and that made him a remarkable person. Many times I heard him say that a man (or woman) can be measured by the importance placed on his or her word. I noticed that he did not say they could be "judged" by their words. I always thought this was a little funny because he was from an era when people "judged" others all the time. If someone was a different religion they were judged. If they belonged to a different political party, they were judged. If they were very rich or very poor, their behaviors were judged. My father was not like this. He accepted people for what they were, even if their behavior or philosophies were different from his. I respected my father a lot, because of his beliefs and his service to others. We should all strive to be as good as he.

One thing he always taught me was that if people can believe what you say, they will continue to have a relationship with you, whether the relationship is of a personal or business nature. As long as people felt you were trustworthy, they would remain in a relationship with you.

My father was a farmer, but he also owned a dirt construction company. Through his dirt construction company he built and repaired waterways, roads, terraces on farmland, etc. Before beginning a project for a client he would sign a contract for the work to be done. A client would know what my dad's work was going to cost and when he would do it.

There were a few times when he experienced cost overruns because he miscalculated the time the project would take. Or, maybe the cost of fuel rose during the time of the construction and made the job more expensive. Maybe some equipment broke down and he incurred significant repair costs while completing the job. But, whatever the reason was for the extra expense incurred for his work, he always did the job for the price he quoted. He said the client needed to know that he could be trusted, if he was ever to be asked to work for them again. Wouldn't it be nice if builders felt that way today?

His philosophy worked well because he was always busy. Land owners in three surrounding counties often did repeat business with him. And, because he usually quoted correct prices for his work, his business was profitable. People knew he was trustworthy, reliable, honest, etc. – they knew he would do what he contracted to do for the price he quoted.

Throughout my life my subconscious has heard his repeated message. The most important value attributed to a human being is the reliability of his or her word. I have tried to run my businesses by this standard, and my clients have done repeat business with me many times.

When I was in my forties, I also had a business on the side. It was a Rock & Roll/Country band and mostly a hobby for fun. All of the members of the band had other full-time jobs, and the band was primarily a way for us to pay for our toys. Musicians are plagued with an addiction to musical instruments. There is always a new one that must be tried or acquired. Our band earned us enough money to accumulate more musical equipment. Some of us played in church bands, so we could use our new toys in that venue, as well.

My father's admonitions to always keep my word even carried over to my music avocation. You see, even after booking a gig, most musicians will cancel if they get a better monetary offer for the same night. For club owners, this is challenging. They have to scramble to find a replacement band at the last moment, and good bands are usually already booked.

My band always completed a contract with the club and upheld our end of the contract. It was tough sometimes because we would get an offer of a gig paying a lot more money. But, we honored our contract. As a result, club owners knew we were reliable. They had no hesitation about booking us.

Because we were good and reliable, we often had gigs booked more than a year in advance. We even performed some nights when a member of the group was sick. We had backup musicians who knew our sets. Our musicians carried union cards so they were all very talented. Because the club owners knew they could count on us to be there when we were supposed to, they even recommended us for higher-paying private parties when their customers asked for it. Rarely did a weekend pass without us having a gig. If we wanted some time off, we had to schedule it on our calendars. All of the band musicians knew that for the long run, we made more money by being regularly booked.

My business and band activities helped re-inforce my father's training in other endeavors. At age forty, I interviewed with a pension administration company in Kansas City. I owned a home in Topeka at the time. The real estate market was a little soft so the owner of the pension administration company was concerned about hiring me. He was worried about my longevity with his company if it took several months to sell my house. He asked me, "Steve, what will happen if it takes a while for you to sell your house and another company in Topeka offers you a job. How do I know you won't take the Topeka job? If that happens, and you take the job, I will have spent money to train you without getting an appropriate return."

My response was, "I completely understand your dilemma and want to set your mind at ease. I am interested in this job and will guarantee you that if you give me this job I will not talk to another employer for at least 24 months. By then, I should have sold my house and will be living in Kansas City." He agreed to hire me. My credentials fit his organization, and the organization was what I was looking for, too.

It's funny how life throws challenges at us. It took about ten months to sell my house. In the meantime, I commuted from Topeka to Kansas City every day. I commuted because I could not afford to make payments on two houses at the time. I even hit a deer at 5:45 AM one morning on my way to work. When that happened, did I think about how lucky I was that I wasn't hurt? No. I was so busy at the time that my first thought was: Boy, this sure screws up my day!

Since my commute was one hour and fifteen minutes to and from work, I knew every song on the radio and every news item on NPR radio. I played hard rock music to wake up on the way to work and classical music on the way home to lower my blood pressure. I knew every tree and flower along the way. There were side benefits though. I enjoyed so many beautiful golden sunrises and sunsets. I was blessed to come over a hill and see the trees in the valley east of Lawrence, Kansas peeking over the ground fog with the golden sun reflecting off the fog. However, by the time ten months had passed, I was really tired of the commute.

What also made the trips a challenge was that I could have ended this commute four months after starting with the pension company. A trust department in Topeka had asked me to join them and work with the pension plans for which the trust department handled the investments. But, I had made a promise to the owner of the pension company. Fortunately, I recalled my father's training and honored my commitment to my new employer. I had told him I would not even talk to another employer for two years. I never mentioned the trust department job to my new employer, even though I was involved in two and one-half hours of commuting every day.

I did not find out until a few months later how fortunate I was to have honored my word and stayed with my Kansas City employer. One night after I returned home to Topeka, I turned on the TV to watch the local news. My time was so limited that about all I had time for was fixing a sandwich or bowl of soup and watching the news before going to bed. I had to go to bed early because I would be rising at 4:00 AM to get ready for the morning commute.

I'm sure my mouth was agape as I watched the news story unfold. People from the pension trust division that had tried to hire me in Topeka were being led from the building in handcuffs. If I had taken the job there, I'm sure I would have been in handcuffs, too. I understand there are circumstances in which people find joy from being in handcuffs, but I am sure none of them are appealing to me. I would feel confined and my claustrophobia would not respond well. My father's training had paid off big-time. By honoring my word to my new employer I was not subjected to the embarrassment of wearing handcuffs on local TV. Not everyone shown in the news story was guilty but they were all initially led out in police jewelry, and I wasn't one of them. Hooray!

I always tell business owners and sales reps that their clients will tell their friends about them. This actually applies to all people (not just clients) and their friends. If you cheat people, they will tell their friends about it. If you treat them with respect and honor their needs with the right solution, they will tell their friends about you. It is totally up to you regarding what they will tell their friends about you. If you want to get referrals, you need to have integrity in your dealings with them. THE VALUE OF YOUR WORD

DETERMINES HOW LONG YOUR RELATIONSHIPS WILL LAST, AND PROBABLY HOW PROFITABLE YOUR ENDEAVORS WILL BE.

THE WHOLE ≠ SOME OF THE PARTS

My father was a wheat farmer living on the plains of Kansas, and was a mechanical genius. He could look at a piece of machinery and know immediately how it functioned. He could even tell if parts from one machine (even if they were different brands) would work on another. I saw him visit with the owner of a road construction salvage yard about a work bull tractor. The work bull was a model of tractor built by Massey Ferguson. The work bull was designed for moving dirt. It came with a mounted loader. Eventually, the Massey Ferguson company was merged with the Massey Harris manufacturing company.

"What's wrong with that work bull?" my father inquired.

The salvage yard owner said, "The transmission is ruined and they don't make this model anymore. Therefore, I cannot get a replacement transmission."

My father pointed at it. "May I take a closer look at it?"

"Sure," said the salvage yard owner, "Just be careful."

Dad walked over to the machine, crawled under it, took out a notepad from his shirt pocket, wrote down a few numbers, and walked back to the owner. "If I was interested in that machine, what would it cost me?"

"It's really only worth scrap value now. So, I'll let you have it for $100."

"Thanks," said my dad. "I'll let you know if I'm interested."

I rode with Dad to another salvage yard that acquired farm tractors. "May I look at some of your old Massey Harris tractors?" He asked. The proprietor told him he could look at anything he wanted to. Dad spent about an hour searching among the rusty tractor carcasses until he found what he wanted. Meantime, I played king of the dead tractors nearby.

When dad returned to the proprietor he asked what it would cost to buy the transmission from a specific model in the yard.

"I'll let you have it for $100."

"Will you remove it for me?" asked my father.

"I'd be happy to," said the proprietor. "When do you want it?"

"If we come back in an hour after lunch, would you be able to have it ready for us?"

"I'll get a team on it right away." Normally my father would have waited a couple of days but this salvage yard was three hours from our house and dad did not want to have to drive back there. We came back after lunch and the transmission was ready. After it was loaded into the back of dad's truck, we headed home.

Dad called about the work bull and was told that it was still available. Pulling a trailer behind his truck he returned to the first salvage yard and bought the work bull.

Dad unloaded the work bull in his machine shed and began to remove the old transmission so he could affix the new one. Three days later his project was completed. The transmission had been attached. It fit like a glove. All the gears meshed together. He started the work bull and drove it around the farmyard. Everything worked perfectly. His total investment in the machine was $200 and a couple of days of labor at that point. He spent a few more dollars on a couple of cans of spray paint and painted the machine. When he finished painting it, it looked new. He advertised it in the regional newspaper for $2,200, and within the week he had a buyer. He had made $2,000 profit.

Because my dad was mechanically skilled, we often had various machines awaiting repairs. One such device in his collection was the motor from a lawnmower. It had been in Dad's parts shed so long that I assumed it was never going to be repaired. My dad was just too busy to spend time rebuilding it.

So, at age 12, I decided to help my dad by fixing the lawnmower motor myself. I had never undertaken any task like this before. What I soon discovered is that mechanical ability is not something one inherits through genetics. I took the engine apart, fixed what I thought was the problem, and then reassembled the motor. When I was done the motor looked complete, but I had a few parts left over. Obviously, they were important parts because the engine never ran again. I did not say anything about it, but a couple of weeks later my father discovered the incomplete engine. He wanted answers. I gave them to him. He wasn't happy about it but did not rebuke me. I think he chocked it up as a learning experience for me. That was one of the first times that I recognized that I would need to pursue another profession. When I was finished with the lawnmower motor, it did not work. It needed to have all of the missing parts to run. The whole (a functioning motor) did not equal just "some" of the parts.

When I was a teenager I happily cheered for my high school's basketball team. We won almost every game, but one stands out to this day. We knew we would undoubtedly beat the team we were going to play on Tuesday night, but it ended up being a slaughter. So many of the players on the other team had fouled out of the game that they played the last quarter with only four team members. When you have a full team and the other team is short a player, it's easy to win. Eventually, our coach pulled our fifth player and we watched four-on-four basketball. It takes a whole team to compete, and the other team did not have a whole team. Again, the whole was not equal to "some" of its parts.

And, a couple of years ago my wife taught me a lesson about women's fashion. She located a plaid suit that was primarily shades of brown. But, approximately every six inches was a reddish-orange line that ran vertically around the suit. It looked beautiful on her, and she bought it. She was not happy with it though. She said she "required" a pair of shoes that matched the reddish-brown stripe.

She decided to continue shopping for the necessary shoes. I accompanied her on her shopping venture. Her goal was to find a pair of reddish-orange shoes to match the stripe in the suit. I was not aware of the importance of coordinating one's attire in such detail. We went to more stores than I could count that day, but we finally found the right pair of shoes. What made her even happier was that the store had her size. After we left the shoe store, I asked her why it was so important to have the shoes. She answered, "Because the outfit was not complete until the shoes were added. The shoes made the ensemble whole. An outfit is not complete unless it has all of the necessary parts."

Some of you may have heard me talk about how I used to play guitar with a band. Most gigs were within two hours of our homes. We practiced to attain a quality sound and usually we were booked more than a year into the future. To produce our quality performances it was imperative that all the band members show up to the gigs. Unfortunately, we had a drummer that marched to the beat of a different drum (pun intended). One night he showed up in time for our second set. To play the first set, our bass guitar player – a very talented musician – stood behind the drums with one foot on the bass drum pedal and the other on the high-hat pedal. He played bass and drums simultaneously. He slapped the strings on his bass to establish a beat, too. We actually sounded pretty good, but we did not sound the same as the "whole" band regularly did. We needed all of the parts, not just "some" of the parts.

So, how do these stories connect with those of us in the financial planning arena? Let me use a real financial planning case to illustrate the connection.

I was working with a couple that owned three local jewelry stores.

They had been in business for more than forty years and were highly successful. People flocked to their stores because they were known for quality products at low prices. Also, this couple thoroughly enjoyed their work. Nothing made them happier than helping a young couple in love pick out just the right engagement ring. Clients did not know it, but sometimes this couple cut their profit margin on an engagement ring to help a young man purchase a ring that made his girl's eyes sparkle. People would drive from all over the state to purchase items from their store.

In their personal lives the couple was frugal. Their jewelry stores generated substantial profits, and they had invested the profits in more businesses and property (e.g., stocks, buildings, land, etc.). Consequently, they had amassed a sizeable estate. They had read articles about the impact of estate taxes and knew they might have an estate tax issue. They wanted to discuss their estate issues and how to manage them. They called me to assist them.

My process with them was the same two-step approach I usually employ. In the first step I gathered facts. We filled out forms listing their assets, goals, desires for heirs, and the like. Then, I took the information back to my office to enter the data into financial planning software models. Because they had significant assets and no desire to ever retire, we did not need to focus on the retirement model. The financial planning software indicated that they had more than enough money for retirement. The main model they wanted to see was the estate planning model. I called them to set up a follow up meeting when I was finished with the analysis. They came to my office a couple of weeks later.

I showed them the mathematical model displaying the impact of estate taxes and inheritance taxes. They were concerned that Uncle Sam would get such a large share. We discussed options they could use to reduce taxes, including the use of gifting to family members, charitable gifts, various trusts, and the use of life insurance to replace the loss from the taxes to which their property was exposed. They had already had discussions with their attorney, so they liked many of the ideas I presented. He had mentioned many of the same options to them. After my presentation the wife asked, "Could I ask another question regarding your analysis?"

"Of course you can," I said, "I want you to have all the information you need to make the right decision. What else would you like to know?"

She hesitated. She looked like she was afraid she would offend me with her question. I assured her she could ask anything she wanted. She asked, "What happens to these numbers if we have more assets than we indicated?"

I needed a little clarification of what she was asking. "If you are worried about your assets continuing to grow, causing these numbers to be currently understated, we will cover that by periodically preparing an update to your file. Usually, this is done at least every two years but it can be done more frequently if your assets are growing pretty fast. Changes in tax laws also will impact the results of our analysis. If the tax laws change, we will need to reevaluate their impact on your estate. These new analyses are provided as part of our ongoing client services package."

She took a deep breath and said, "That is not what I was asking."

"I'm sorry," I said, "I guess I jumped the gun on you. What was it that you wanted to know?"

"I'm a little embarrassed," she said. "I know you went to a lot of work on this analysis, and I know it is not correct. It cannot be correct."

I suspected that I knew the answer to my next question because I had experienced this before with other conservative clients. "Why would it not be correct?"

"Because we might not have given you complete facts about our situation," she replied. "We might have understated the total assets we own on your forms."

"If the amounts you gave me were understated, the results showing estate taxes will also be understated. Don't worry too much if you think you slightly understated your holdings. People often guess low on the values of their property. Deep down it is hard for most people to realize that inflation has caused that much growth in what they own."

Her face was a little flushed. She felt guilty over the data they had provided. She continued, "It's not about making low guesses. We simply did not tell you about everything we own. We have a hard time telling people what we are worth. Some people might think we cheat them in our business practices if they knew how much we are worth. The truth is that we have simply made excellent investments that have done well. We have a stockbroker handling an account for us, and we did not tell you about that sizeable account."

I responded, "I have many clients who have money that is managed by other people. I don't tell clients that they need to invest all of their money through me. A request like that is beyond their comfort level. Also, many have built a friendship with another advisor, and they do not want that relationship affected. If clients are having great success with another money manager, that's great. However, I cannot produce accurate financial analyses if I don't know about those assets. Do you think the assets you are talking about would have much impact on the results of my analysis?"

"I know they would have a big effect on the results because the account is sizeable."

Curiosity got the best of me. "Would you like to tell me what that amount is?" I asked.

"Five million dollars," she said.

In light of this new information maintaining my composure was challenging. I'm sure my face showed my displeasure. I had devoted a lot of time preparing their report and now the numbers were really off. I did not outwardly display any anger. I simply stated, "Well, the report I prepared will significantly understate your estate tax need. The primary problem is that the estate tax tables are progressive like the income tax. The higher your assets, the higher the percentage of estate taxes that you will incur."

She added, "We are impressed with the type of work you do, but we would like to see a more accurate representation of our estate tax exposure. Is there any way we can get you to rerun our numbers if we give you corrected data?" She looked at me with pleading eyes.

"I can certainly redo your analysis," I said. "I'm sure you can relate to what I am about to say. I may need to charge a fee for these additional calculations. Just like in your shop, time is a valuable commodity in ours. You've undoubtedly experienced a similar scenario in your stores. You've probably had a new customer ask you to create jewelry using a certain design and, after seeing it, wants it altered. In those circumstances you may have to charge extra labor for the requested changes. So, if you are willing to cover the costs of the reruns, we can prepare a new report for you." They agreed. (I didn't charge them any extra fee because they ended up becoming excellent clients.) With corrected data, we were able to show their true need. Without it, our analysis was incomplete.

I cannot emphasize this enough – the most important process in serving your clients is gathering "all" the facts you can so you can formulate solutions that resolve their problems. It is important to explain this to your prospects and clients at the beginning of your relationship. Incomplete data will produce erroneous calculation results. It's the old "garbage in, garbage out" adage. But the solutions you propose need more than just numerical figures or estimates to be useful. You need to incorporate the psychological factors, as well. They need to be able to sleep at night. You need to design questions that get to the psychology behind their goals.

You need them to explain their visions for the future to you. You want them to describe how they plan to spend their time in retirement. You need to ask questions that reveal what they feel.

Perhaps some of the following questions will serve as examples.

What future do you envision for your children when they complete high school? If something happens to you today, and you look back from the great beyond in ten years to see your family, how have their lives been? What future do you see for you and your family? Do you think your children will want to take over your business? What will your business look like in five years? What will it look like in ten years? What will it look like if something happens to you?

You can purchase books that give you lists of questions to ask your clients. You can also ask other sales reps about the questions they ask their clients and prospects. And, if you pay attention to the approaches you use, you will learn which questions have been effective for you. You want your client's analysis to represent the "whole" picture. As you gather data from your clients, always remember that the whole is not equal to "some" of the parts. Clarify your client's answers with questions seeking more details.

A PIECE OF CANDY IS BETTER THAN NO CANDY AT ALL

As a financial planner I have learned much about people and their behavior patterns. One prominent lesson I have learned is that most people have no clue how their take-home pay is being spent. At the end of the year there is usually a fairly large amount of money for which they cannot account. Occasionally, I meet a client that uses Quicken, or some similar software, to manage his or her money. Often, these people can tell me even where there pennies are spent. But, these types of record keepers are rare.

It seems like the more income a family has, the more removed they are from their spending habits. I've had doctors making more than $50,000 per month come to me for help because they "cannot make ends meet." I found this surprising because, at the same time, I owned a rental property with a single mother who had five children, and she was able to "get by" on $1500 per month.

How does this situation occur? How is it possible to earn a lot of money and not know where it goes? Often, it happens because the family does not pay attention to how they are spending the cash in their purses and wallets. They also reason that their income level is large enough that they can easily cover their spending habits. But, anyone can spend more than he or she earns. Even famous celebrities with huge incomes occasionally declare bankruptcy, because they spent too much on the wrong things. Perhaps a personal example will shed light on this occurrence.

A few years ago a financial advisor asked me to meet with him and his clients. The purpose of the meeting was for me to gather facts to enable me to prepare a detailed financial plan. The advisor was an excellent producer and knew his product lines well, but he had never prepared a financial plan. He felt these clients needed a thorough financial analysis. His clients earned around $200,000 of annual household income, but they needed help developing strategies for retirement. We had them complete fact-gathering forms before our joint meeting.

Surprisingly, they had done an excellent job of completing the forms. Many times when I ask clients to complete financial data, the results are less than stellar. While the clients were not able to recognize any patterns from just completing the forms, they had done the required homework for me. I gave the forms a quick glance and asked, "Are you aware that there is a $16,000 difference between what you are taking home in disposable income and what you are spending each year? Would you know where that $16,000 is going?" They were stunned. They had not noticed there was such a large variance.

My question created an immediate argument. They were

suppressing the argument because they had visitors, but they were clearly concerned. This was a sizeable amount of money to go missing each year. If they had that money, they could do so many things with it. Each blamed the other for his or her wanton spending habits.

I interrupted their discussion. "Do either of you ever go to an ATM to withdraw funds?" Both agreed that this was almost a daily experience. I wanted to explore this a little more. "Why do you make the withdrawals, and how is the money spent?"

The wife responded first. "It happens for a number of reasons. For example, every time someone at the office has a special event, (e.g., a birthday, a childbirth, retirement, etc.), someone comes around to collect money for a gift. I can't ask them to take a credit card or a check. The building has an ATM on the lower level so I go to it and make a withdrawal. If my department wants to get together after work at a local restaurant I get cash to chip in my share at the end of the night. Additionally, I am trying to keep the balances on my credit cards down because interest rates are high, so if I decide to shop after work, I might get cash to do that."

The husband echoed her comments." I, too, encounter collections at the office for the same types of events. Also, if I go to lunch with other office personnel I retrieve cash to cover my share. Then, there is the occasional payment of a lost wager from a golf game or when my sports teams loses. I guess I just didn't realize how often we withdraw cash."

I decided it was time to diffuse the situation. "You are not that different from a lot of other successful couples. They, too, have significant amounts of cash expenditures they cannot account for at the end of the year. We'll run a mathematical analysis first and then talk about ways to get this under control. One other question I have has to do with some of your assets. I noticed that you have over $330,000 in Certificates of Deposits. Is there a reason for this?"

The husband answered. "I guess those would be mine. I'm pretty conservative so I don't want to be in stocks. Interest rates right now are pretty high so I'm happy with the return I'm getting. My wife is more aggressive and takes more investment risk."

"If we could show you another type of investment that is considered conservative and has similar returns, but offers really good tax advantages would you entertain moving some of your CD money into it?"

"Well, I do get a little tired coming up with the taxes on the CD interest at the end of the year. I'll need convincing, but I am willing to listen. I want to get our finances under control, especially since I know there is $16,000 per year that goes missing."

We left with the forms, and I went back to my office to complete a detailed financial plan. The advisor on the case scheduled a follow-up appointment a couple of weeks later. I had discussed the CDs with the advisor. I explained that this client was not using the CD money and was simply saving it for retirement so tying it up in an annuity should not be a problem. I mentioned that the CD money could grow faster if it was not exposed to taxes. The product I thought might be of interest to the client was a nonqualified deferred annuity. The advisor said he would explore the annuity product line available to him to sell.

A couple of weeks later at our meeting, the advisor and I sat down with the clients. We were on one side of the table. They were on the other. I had prepared enough copies of my analysis for each person to have his or her own copy. Over the next hour I went through the analysis. It did not provide any surprises. It showed a need to put more money away for retirement. They agreed with the results, but did not know where the additional investment funds would come from. I suggested a couple of ways the money could become available.

One source would be finding the missing $16,000. While there would always be a need for some cash, we might be able to consider ways to reduce their withdrawals. We explained that it was probably time for the clients to create a monthly budget. It would require a little work, but they were willing to provide the labor. After all, we were talking about a sizeable annual amount that magically disappeared. The clients were computer literate so we discussed software that could help with the process.

The second recommendation I made was to reduce the taxation on his CD interest. I explained the virtues of annuities. The money being paid annually in taxes could stay in his investments and grow for use in retirement. While he was intrigued by these products, he had never owned one and was unsure how safe his money would be if he put it in the annuity. Right now, he knew his money was protected by the FDIC because it was held by a bank.

I explained that there were some limits on FDIC coverage so he might want to find out if all his money was protected. I mentioned that I was fairly certain that some of it was not. I also reminded him that the interest on his CDs was subject to income taxation each year. Because of their annual income levels, their tax rate was pretty high. Eliminating these annual taxes would keep more money working for them. Without the reduction of taxes each year, more money would be available for growth. A larger amount would be available for retirement income. I further suggested they could call the state insurance department to get more information on annuities and their safety.

As part of the fact gathering process, the husband had provided a list of his Certificates of Deposit. The list showed the interest amounts being paid and the maturity date connected to each CD. When I was done with my presentation the advisor took out his copy of the CD list and said, "Okay, now it's time to discuss moving your CDs into an annuity." He showed a product to the client and laid out the application to enable the client to surrender the CDs and invest the money in the annuity.

The client leaned back in his chair, crossed his arms, and said, "I'm not going to do that. Some of these CDs have maturity dates a few years into the future. There is a substantial penalty for early withdrawal. It would cost me a lot of money to make the switch."

"But you will recoup those costs over the years because your account will grow faster. The interest won't be subject to annual taxation. Also, by purchasing the annuity you can guarantee that you will have a retirement income that lasts for your entire life. You really should move the money into CDS."

I could tell the client had erected a wall of resistance. His body language showed that he was closed to the idea of moving his CD money. He added, "I'm familiar with CDs. I've owned them for a long time. But I have never owned an annuity. I'm not comfortable moving all my CD money to a product I know nothing about."

The advisor continued to press the client about his need to move the money. Each minute the advisor talked, the client's resistance grew. It was obvious that no sale would be made today if this technique was continued. I sat there and watched until the client turned to me and asked, "If you were in my situation would you move my CD money to an annuity?"

Now, I have always tried to treat people the way I would want to be treated. My parents told me about the "Golden Rule" many times when I was growing up. I responded honestly to his question. "No, I would not. Some of your CDs have maturity dates several years into the future. If you surrender them now you will incur enough surrender charges that you will get back less than you invested in them." The advisor was obviously not happy with me. He did not realize that he was running down a dead-end path by putting pressure on the client.

I continued, "What I noticed is that you have three CDs that will mature in the next two weeks. What I suggest is that you move only those three to an annuity right now. You could surrender the CDs and write a check for the annuity. Tax-wise this won't be any different than the situation you are currently in. You will be paying taxes on the interest earned on the CDs at the end of the year anyway. If you surrender the CDs you will still pay taxes on the interest earned to the point of surrender. We can complete the application today, if you like, and when you surrender your CDs you can write us a check for the amount you get as the first premium. At the end of the year, when you get your IRS Form 1099-INT on your CDs and you don't get one on your annuity, you'll see the value the annuity offers."

I added, "You also mentioned that you did not know anything about annuities. You will have plenty of time to research them. Your CD money will not be available for a couple of weeks. Also, the annuity product will have a 'free look' period. This means you will have 20 days to review the contract after it is provided to you. If, after reviewing the annuity, you decide you do not want it you can get your money back and return it to a new CD. Why don't we take the first step in the process and complete the annuity application now. It only takes a few minutes."

The advisor completed the application and handed it to the client to sign. He signed it. I emphasized he should contact the state insurance department with his annuity questions. Then we left.

I knew the advisor was probably going to express his disappointment with my approach when we got into the car. I was right. He blurted, "You just cost me a $330,000 annuity sale."

I let him vent. When he was done, I asked, "Did you hear him say repeatedly that he was not going to move the CD money? Did you notice his body language? You were clearly on the path to no sale. Now you at least have a sale for $75,000. Over the next few years you'll get the rest. However, the most important result is that you kept this client. He was getting annoyed. It would not have surprised me if he told us to get lost if you had continued the approach you were using."

I said, "When I was a small child, my mother would use techniques to foster good behavior in me. She would give me a small piece of candy as a reward. I think I already practiced my sales techniques with her back then, because I would try to persuade her to give me more than one piece. She would say, 'Remember, a piece of candy is better than no candy at all. And, by limiting how much candy you get now, we'll have candy left for later'. Whether the reward was ice cream, cake, pie, or a brownie, she always reminded me that a piece was better than nothing. It's the same thing with the financial planning process. We don't always get all of a client's money in our first appointment, and sometimes we shouldn't because it is not in the client's best interest. Sometimes they feel more comfortable having some of their money with another advisor. Our first step with a client should be to grow the relationship. We want to make sure we are able to support their financial needs in the future.

"Too often, we are concerned about 'closing' a sale. This technique works well for car sales reps and appliance sales personnel, because the probability of seeing the purchaser again is small. They need to make the sale now. They need to 'close' the deal. The products they sell last long enough that the sales rep will possibly be at another employer by the time the buyer returns. As a financial advisor or planner, our goal should be on 'opening' a relationship with a client. We want to be able to serve a client's needs for years. We want to help with their insurance needs. We want to structure their retirement plans. We hope to help build the education fund their children need. This 'opening' process must be pursued from the start. It's not about making one sale. It's about multiple sales as we serve the client's long-term needs."

Let's look at another story that was related to me by my friend, Don. He was an excellent sales rep with years of serving his clients. This story took place early in his career. He had both a CLU (Chartered Life Underwriter), and a CFP (Certified Financial Planner) designation.

Don is dedicated to providing the right solutions for his client's problems. He received a phone call from a young father, Jack, to discuss life insurance. He arranged a meeting with the young family. Jack, age 29, was the sole breadwinner in the family. He and his wife, Amy (age 27) had three children under the age of 7.

Don explained that he used a two-step process with most of his clients. He applied the same technique in this case. For step one, he gathered facts. He found out the family's goals, what assets were available, what assets were needed, and calculated any shortfalls that needed correcting. He returned a couple of weeks later with the analysis. He concentrated on the life insurance portion of the analysis because that is what the prospect had said was important at this time. The analysis showed a need of $335,000 of life insurance. Coupled with social security benefits the insurance amount would provide adequate funds to take care of the family should Jack die. Unfortunately, Jack could not purchase a whole life policy for this amount because the premium amount was simply more than he could afford.

Don had already known this when he prepared the analysis. To make sure the young family would have enough life insurance, Don designed a life insurance policy that was a combination of whole life insurance with a term insurance rider. He was able to get the $335,000 needed at a price the young family could afford. Don showed a policy illustration to the husband.

"My father always told me that if I bought life insurance I should always buy ten-pay life," Jack responded."

"I know why you would be interested in ten-pay life," said Don. "After 10 years, no more premiums are required on the policy. Unfortunately, when all of the premiums on a whole life policy are paid in only ten years, the premium amount goes up. With the monthly premium you told me you can afford, it is impossible to buy the $335,000 you need. We are probably looking at somewhere between $25,000 and $50,000 of coverage and that simply will not take care of your family for very long."

The young man was insistent. "I want a ten-pay life policy," he repeated.

Don repeated, "If I sell you a ten-pay life policy and something happens to you, I will never forgive myself for not selling you enough insurance to take care of your family. Do you realize how long the proceeds from a ten-pay life policy will last? Your family will run out of money in a couple of years."

Again, the young man said, "I want a ten-pay life insurance policy. If you won't sell it to me, I'll find someone who will."

Don had recently completed his CLU and CFP designations. He knew that he needed to treat his clients properly. He knew he needed to do the right thing. Moreover, he was also worried about legal ramifications from Jack's family if they did not have enough money to live on. "I'm sorry," Don said, "but, I simply cannot sell you the wrong product for your family."

The young man's face flushed as he stated, "Then you can get the hell out of my house."

Don was stunned. He had not expected such a bold reaction. He apologized to Jack, picked up his materials and his briefcase, and exited through the front door. He felt bad the conversation had gone the way it did, but he knew he had done the right thing.

A couple of weeks later Don attended the local financial planning association meeting. Even though he was still somewhat new to the industry and the association, he had belonged long enough to know many of the members. His friend, Fred, approached. They engaged in small talk about the weather, how their families were doing, and what was happening in their businesses. Then Fred said, "Oh, I forgot. I want to thank you for the business you gave me the other night."

Don was confused. He did not remember sending any business Fred's way. "What do you mean, Fred? I didn't send any business to you. You're a good guy but I usually can serve my own clients. Also, I don't think you offer any products that I don't offer."

Don could tell that Fred was teasing him a little. "Don, you didn't directly send me any business, but you indirectly provided a new client for me." Fred reminded Don about his meeting with Jack, the young man that wanted a ten-pay life insurance policy. "Do you remember him?" Fred asked.

Don replied. "I sure do. It's hard to forget someone that kicked you out of his house. But, Fred, what did you sell him?"

Fred responded, "I sold him a ten-pay life insurance policy."

Don couldn't believe it. Fred was an upstanding member in the association and he had sold his client an inadequate life insurance amount. "Didn't you explain to him that the insurance amount would be inadequate to provide very long for his family?"

"I repeated it to him a couple of times, but he was insistent that he only wanted to pay ten years of premiums. When he would not relent, I wrote the insurance."

"Aren't you worried about what might happen if he dies? His family might bring legal action."

"I did worry about that. That's why I had Jack and Amy affix their signatures to an agreement stating that I had explained the shortfall to them."

"Fred, you know you did not sell him the right product. How can you live with yourself?"

"Don, if something happens to this young man at least his wife will get some insurance. If he had died the night after you met with him she would not have gotten any life insurance proceeds. Also,

Jack is now a client of mine and that's statistically important. Statistics show that most people purchase life insurance at least five times in their lives. Because he is now my client, I have four more times to try to get him to buy the right product. By taking the approach you took, you have no future chances to help him get the right coverage. I've learned that sometimes I have to do what the client wants so he or she will become a client. Then I'll have a chance to help him or her do what is really needed."

A piece of candy is better than no candy at all.

LET ME TELL YOU WHY I DON'T NEED…

Because I hold a QPA Designation (Qualified Pension Administrator) from the American Society of Pension Practitioners and Actuaries, I am sometimes called upon by financial planners to help them with an employer's retirement plan. Usually, this involves designing a retirement plan formula that meets the employer's objectives. I accompanied Glen on one such case.

Glen's client was a small partnership owned by two brothers. The business had around ten employees. Both brothers were basically benevolent toward their employees. They took care of them. The employee benefit package was good. Employees were offered health insurance, dental insurance, disability insurance, and a retirement plan called a SEP (Simplified Employee Pension plan).

We were meeting with the partners to review the SEP and determine if a better plan was available for the business. Actually, we only met with one of the partners. They did not feel it was important enough for both of them to attend. After all, they already had the SEP and they were happy with it.

We were escorted to their business's meeting room and were seated at a table that looked like one you would see in a corporate boardroom. Obviously, the room was used for employee and client meetings. Maximum capacity around the walnut table was around sixteen.

We sat across the table from one of the partners named Bill. After introductions, small talk about the weather, and comments about the local baseball teams, Bill leaned back in his chair like he was trying not to catch a cold from me, crossed his arms with his hands folded underneath, and said, "Let me tell you why I don't need a different retirement plan." Then, he explained the values of the SEP.

Later, I would explain to Glen that I usually expected some resistance from a prospect, but it was rare to encounter it before I had even spoken one word. All the signs of a potential struggle were there. His body language clearly indicated that he had no interest in what I was about to say. He was leaning away from me. In fact, he was as far away from me as he could get without tipping over his chair or leaving the room. Secondly, his arms were crossed and wrapped tightly around him. He was clearly protecting himself from the bad pension guy. Thirdly, he abruptly told me he did not need anything I offered. He was happy with the plan he had and did not want his happiness disturbed.

Glen had already forewarned me that this might happen. Bill was already a personal client of Glen's and had been for a few years. Bill had life insurance and investments through Glen. His investments had done well and Bill respected Glen's talents.

One technique I often use to diffuse a negative response from a prospect is agreement. In other words, I agree with him or her. I decided to try that approach. "Bill," I said, "Glen told me what type of plan your business has and gave me an employee census. I ran the numbers to see what the allocations look like. Is this a good example of how the SEP allocations look?"

Bill took the example from me. He squinted as he looked at the numbers, then he said "Yeah, that's almost exactly how the contributions are allocated."

"Well, Bill, after seeing the allocation breakdown I ran a profit-sharing plan analysis to see what those allocations would look like. Here's the allocation under it." I handed him this example. "As you can see, the allocations are virtually the same. After doing this analysis I came to the same conclusion you did. For allocation purposes, you don't need a profit-sharing plan." It looked like his chest expanded with pride. A profit-sharing plan enables you to include a vesting schedule whereas the SEP requires the employees to be fully vested immediately. But the extra cost of plan administration for the profit sharing plan is probably more than the vesting cost under the SEP.

"Then, Bill, I decided to integrate these plans with social security. Under this formula, your business gets to recognize that it is paying social security costs for the employees already, and an adjustment is made in the allocations to reflect that. Often, this formula slants a little more toward the partners because the social security contribution amounts for the highly-paid employees are limited by the taxable wage base. In other words, social security taxes are not paid on salaries above certain limits. Since social security benefits are based on the wages used in determining the required contributions, higher paid employees experience a little reverse discrimination. As a percentage of their salaries, their social security benefits will be smaller than benefits for lower paid employees. The tax code allows an adjustment to make the total retirement benefits reflect more equity."

"Here's what the numbers look like when I integrated both the SEP and the profit-sharing plan. As you can see, they are very close again. Thus, it would be difficult to justify the profit-sharing administration costs. The SEP would be the plan of choice."

"Now, Bill. I have been working with retirement plans through many tax changes. I am familiar with the contribution allocations that different formulas can produce. Therefore, I decided to see how a more sophisticated plan would work. I ran an example showing an age-weighted 401(k) plan." (I explained how this type of formula usually resulted in a larger allocation for older, higher paid employees, which represented the category the brothers were in).

This whole time that I was showing the examples, Bill maintained his stance. His arms were tightly crossed and he was leaning dangerously back in his chair. I slid the example across the table. It showed how the contributions for the employees would remain essentially the same under this formula as they were under the SEP; however, the profit sharing allocations and deferrals for the brothers more than doubled. He leaned forward and picked up the example to study it. If you understand body language, you know this was a very positive sign. I had piqued his interest. The questions began to flow. An hour later he called his brother into the meeting. Together they decided to replace the SEP with the 401(k) plan. Administration costs were low enough to make the 401(k) a viable solution.

Did I know the partners would respond to my example? Of course I didn't. Glen had told me these owners were benevolent toward their employees. I did not know if the formula that would slant contributions to the brothers would be appealing to them. Most times a shift like that is. It certainly was in this case, but I had no indicators to believe the formula would appeal to them. Sometimes, I get an indication from the facts that are provided to me. Let's look at another example.

I met with two different employers on the same day to discuss retirement plans for their businesses. The first business owner was truly benevolent toward his employees. He valued their contributions to the bottom line. You could see how he felt by looking at the census showing employee salaries. The difference between the owner's salary and the next employee's salary was small. In fact, all of the salary amounts were fairly close. For this owner, a plan that treated the employer and his employees equitably was proposed and accepted. The contribution percentages were the same for all of the employees.

When I looked at the employee census for the next corporation, I knew immediately that a different approach would be needed. It, too, was a small business (only 5 employees). But, the employee census revealed much about the psychology of the owner. His salary was $575,000. The next employee's salary was $78,000. To appeal to this owner, a plan would need to slant most of the contribution allocation to the owner. We were able to use a combination defined benefit pension plan (slants contributions to older employees) with an age-weighted 401(k). About 94% of the contributions went toward the owner's accounts. He was extremely happy with the formulas.

Another case involved a chiropractor in a small town. I think the town had a population of around 4,000. His practice was the only one in town. There had been other chiropractors but some had retired, some had moved to larger cities, and some had been acquired by this practice. He had a few other licensed chiropractors in his office. He had planned on his son taking over the practice someday, but sadly, his son had been killed in an automobile accident at the age of thirty-two.

He had hired a young chiropractor who was interested in taking over the business when he retired. They had a verbal arrangement. I approached the chiropractor about employing a buy-sell agreement. A buy-sell agreement is a contractual arrangement that requires a deceased owner's heirs or estate to sell his shares to someone else. The other party to the agreement is obligated to buy the deceased's shares. Thus, the heirs are assured (in this case, the wife) that they will receive money to cover their financial needs.

He explained to me that he did not need a buy-sell agreement because he already had an arrangement with the young chiropractor in his practice. (This was his way of saying, "Let me tell you why I don't need..."). The plan was that when the owner of the practice died, became disabled, or retired, the young chiropractor would buy the practice. "I'm sure he is an honorable young man, but what if he doesn't buy the business and provide funds for your wife?"

He looked at me like I was insane. "Why wouldn't he buy the practice? He would have no competition because there are no other practices in town. He will gain a loyal staff, none of whom want the responsibility of owning the practice. The practice will provide a nice income to provide for his family. He'd be silly not to buy it."

"There are a few points you should consider," I said. "First of all, what if something happens to you tonight? Can he come up with the money to purchase the practice? Since he is so young and inexperienced at overseeing the financial affairs of the practice, will he be able to get a loan to buy the business? If he is able to get the loan, will the loan payments put enough pressure on the practice that it will not succeed?

"And, most importantly, are you recognizing the fact that he doesn't have to buy the business at all? All he needs to do, if something happens to you, is open shop across the street. Where are the clients going to get their chiropractic work done? There are no other practices in town. He will get your patients without spending a penny. Now, that might not happen, but it could. It would be a shame to build a practice like yours and not have your heirs receive anything for it. It is so easy to set up a buy-sell arrangement. Then, to assure he has money to buy the business he can purchase a life insurance policy on you. At your death, he must fulfill his part of the agreement, and the life insurance will provide the funds. This makes sure your wife has adequate income." This client must have worried about this for a day or two, because he decided to install the buy-sell arrangement. I'm sure he slept better after it was completed.

When you are visiting with your prospects you need to look for signs revealing what makes him or her tick. Usually you will encounter resistance at some point in the presentation so you need to learn how to understand what the client is saying. You need to learn to read body language. There are many books written about body language and you can find them online. You will be surprised how many signals one's body sends in any communication. It is important to have this knowledge. For example, I've been with reps that are clearly upsetting their prospects, but they did not know it because they could not read the prospect's body language.

The other signs you need to look for are those involving the prospect's communication methods. If the client uses phrases like: "I see," "Let me look into that", etc., you will need to communicate with examples that paint a visual picture. You might describe the mountains in the background of their retirement retreat. You might help them visualize their grandchildren walking across the stage at their college graduation.

When the client uses phrases like, "I hear you," or "Listen to what I have to say," your communication technique will take on a different approach. The example related to the retirement retreat will emphasize the birds singing as they sit on their cabin porch. The inflection of their voices becomes important. What words they emphasize in a sentence indicate a different meaning. Try this experiment: take a sentence and read it placing emphasis on a different word each time you read it. The meaning is changed dramatically with each reading.

Communication success depends on many factors. It's not just about the words that are spoken. It's possible to "listen" to someone but not really "hear" what they are saying. My wife accuses me of stuff like that a lot, or at least I think she mentioned something to that effect.

You cannot be in sales without experiencing resistance. Prospects have many products on which they can spend their money. Knowing how to read your prospect better so you know how they think puts you in a better position to serve their needs. You will be in a better position when you hear your prospect say, "Let me tell you why I don't need..."

KNOWLEDGE

Knowledge can be a double-edged sword. It's important to have knowledge, but it must be the right kind of knowledge. Some knowledge can limit progress. Some knowledge can cause society or an individual to progress more rapidly. Let me explain.

During the medieval ages it was a well-known fact that the world was flat. Anyone with intelligence knew that. In fact, if you did not know that you were considered a heretic and might be punished severely – maybe even put to death. This particular body of knowledge undoubtedly limited world exploration. Why would you set sail too far from land if you were just going to fall off the edge of the planet anyway? Who knows how fast western civilization might have expanded if it were not for this incorrect category of knowledge.

There is a book titled, *They Said It Couldn't be Done* by Victor Boesen. It was published in 1971 so it isn't easy to find, but a thorough search, if you are interested, will reveal available copies from online resources. It is a book about William (Bill) P. Lear. Some of you know him as the developer of the Lear Jet, but he invented many devices. Sometimes he was told that what he was trying to achieve could not be done. Stories about Bill indicate that he was often subjected to obstacles as he tried to develop new products. The biggest obstacles were not always the devices he was trying to construct, but the people who told him the device he was developing could not be created. They kept telling him it could not be done.

Bill Lear was a self-taught genius. He dropped out of school after the eighth grade but continued to study. He was interested in electronic devices. His timing was great because he was discovering electrical techniques in the early 1900s. To further his knowledge he studied the writings of Nikola Tesla, who was considered to be a genius in the realm of electricity. Radios were becoming an extremely popular device in the early part of the twentieth century. They were big, bulky devices, but families would sit around the radio in the evening and listen to music, dramas, comedy, news, etc.

Purportedly, a girlfriend told him and a friend that it would be nice to be able to listen to the radio when they were in the car. He set out to create a radio and battery small enough to fit in an automobile. However, his knowledge limited him. He did not know that it could be mathematically proven that radio coils had to be at least a certain size to produce a quality sound. Electrical engineers could prove it to him. But, he did not have an engineering degree so he did not know it was impossible to produce a small radio coil that would provide a quality sound. The prevalent knowledge was impeding radio progress.

Bill was told his idea would not work. Even his friend, Algot Olson, who loaned Bill $5,000 to build the smaller radio, told him it would not work. Bill persevered and built the radios with the smaller coil in the basement of his mother's house. When he approached Eugene McDonald of Zenith Electronics to demonstrate his new product, he was met with resistance. McDonald could not believe that the quality of Bill's radio would be better than the ones Zenith already offered. After listening to Bill's radio, Zenith placed an order for 50,000 of the units. Prevailing radio knowledge had not limited Bill's progress.

Now, please do not misunderstand what I am saying. I am not opposed to the acquisition of knowledge. What I am trying to state is: Don't let existing knowledge limit your growth or your company's growth. Too often, we are stymied by the "We've always done it this way" mentality. Or, a compliance lawyer who has never thoroughly read the regulations that apply to the procedure we want to use says that the procedure cannot be done. They are not always correct.

You should know that there may be other reasons you are being told not to pursue a business product you want to sell through your company. Perhaps the company's systems cannot do what you ask. Maybe the company simply chooses not to undertake the activity – some markets are just not sufficiently profitable to spend time and money on them. Maybe the regulations are not clear enough for a definitive interpretation.

A good company will choose product lines that help it stay in business. It is certainly okay, though, to have them research whether knowledge (or lack thereof) is the culprit intervening in the pursuit of the product line. Be tactful with your approach. There have been a few times when I was able to help a company alter the rules that had previously existed. If you know that a competitor is pursuing a market that your company is not, you might bring it to your company's attention. But, don't rely on that argument. There are some very aggressive companies out there. Some were so aggressive in prior years that they do not exist anymore. Your company's approach may be the safest.

Please note that I am a big advocate of gaining knowledge. Were that not so, I would not have much of the alphabet following my name (multiple designations). Each of my designations has advanced my abilities to serve clients. Sometimes I have been able to propose solutions other advisors were unable to see, simply because my knowledge base was a little larger. Increasing your knowledge base can do this for you, too. One simple way to be more competitive is to know your product.

Recently, I visited with a car sales rep about features a new model had versus the one I owned. I was amazed at how much detail he knew about the car models. If I asked him what a certain model had that was different than another, he knew the little things like, "The only real difference between this one and that one is that this one has a digital compass and that one does not." Now that is impressive. Knowing these details undoubtedly helps him make an extra sale now and then.

Let me provide a simple example from my financial services experience. This involved an insurance agent who had sold a $1,000,000 life insurance policy to his client. The client had recently passed away. The insurance sale was a suitable sale because the client needed the insurance to take care of his wife after he was gone. The problem came from the fact that the client had named his son as the beneficiary of the policy. The son was a prominent CPA in the community.

The CPA son had amassed enough personal wealth that he did not want the policy's death proceeds added to his net worth. First of all, the additional assets would expose him to more estate and inheritance taxes. Secondly, if something happened to the CPA, he was not sure his family would use the money to take care of his mom. This was important. He wanted his mom to have the money. He told the agent that if he could find a way for the death proceeds to be paid to the mom, the agent would get to handle the $1,000,000 investment and maybe more. The agent and the CPA called me to discuss solutions. They were on a speaker phone.

After they explained the dilemma, I asked, "Did your father name a contingent beneficiary. In other words, if something were to happen to you, is another person named who would have received money?"

The CPA answered, "No. No other beneficiary was indicated on the application copy in the policy. I called the insurance company and they confirmed that no other person was named as a contingent beneficiary. I'm just trying to figure out how we can get the money to my mother without me having to give her a gift. I don't want to use up any of my federal gift tax exclusion by giving her the proceeds. I need as much of the exclusion available for my own assets."

"Mr. CPA," I responded, "There is probably a way to get this done but I need you to investigate a couple of things for me. Do you have a complete copy of the life insurance policy?"

He replied, "I do. Would you like me to read through certain sections of it?"

"First, let me ask you another question. Did your father have a will that might have left everything to your mother?"

"That's what is really funny," he said. "He had a will that left everything to my mom, but when he bought this policy he named me as beneficiary with the idea that I would use it to take care of her. It doesn't make sense that he did it this way."

"Mr. CPA, when you read through your father's policy, check to see if there are provisions that describe what happens when a beneficiary has died before the insured. Sometimes beneficiaries die before the insured does so insurance companies include policy provisions to cover that situation. You will undoubtedly discover that the policy states that if there are no living beneficiaries when the insured dies, the proceeds are paid to the insured's estate."

There was a slight pause. I could tell he was thinking. "How is that going to help in this circumstance? There is a living beneficiary, and it's me."

"There may be a way around that. It's called a 'formal disclaimer.' Virtually every state has a formal disclaimer procedure, and I'll bet yours does, too. If you have a friend who is an estate planning attorney you can ask him or her if your state has one. If so, regulations relating to the disclaimer will describe how you can disclaim the death proceeds. Under this procedure you refuse the death proceeds. You give up your claim. Once a proper disclaimer is created, it's as though you don't exist. It is as though you have died. Then, the proceeds are left to the next beneficiary in line. In this case, there is no other beneficiary so the proceeds default to the policy provision that authorizes the payment to the estate. Since your mom receives all assets of the estate under the will, the death proceeds will go to her. Follow these procedures I have discussed with you. Then, let me know how everything turns out."

Everything turned out great. With the help of an attorney he disclaimed his interest in the death proceeds. The insurance company paid the proceeds to the estate in accordance with the policy provisions. After the estate went through probate the property was transferred to the CPA's mom. The agent got to invest the estate assets and a little more. The CPA was happy. The mom was happy. And, the agent was happy.

The primary knowledge involved in this case was the knowledge of policy provisions. A little estate planning knowledge helped discuss the disclaimer with the client. Other financial advisors had told him there was nothing that could be done. They told him he would have to take the proceeds. Our information helped the CPA accomplish what he wanted. The CPA felt comfortable using the agent on many other cases. He even referred him to some of his clients.

So how do you gain more of the right kind of knowledge? Look to your industry. What sources are available to you? There are many.

Let's look at some resources you can call upon:

- **Mentors** – Most likely you have access to many mentors. Look to associates who have been in your industry for a while. They do not have to be with your company. If you are in sales, find out how the successful sales reps conduct their business. If you are in corporate world, seek out others who have been in your department and who have experienced varying hurdles. Ask questions. Listen to the answers.

- **Books** – Your mentors will undoubtedly know which books offer sage advice. Your company may even furnish copies to you at no charge. Some books will be on target. Some will waste your time. Ask others which ones they found most helpful.

- **Audio Tapes** – Maybe you are not the type to sit down and read a book. Perhaps you have limited time to do so. An audio tape can be listened to while you are driving through rush hour traffic or to see a client. You can even listen to the tape while you are working out at the gym. Again, ask others for recommendations or check out the reviews online.

- **Video Tapes** – I have found video tapes to be helpful when I was studying difficult topics, especially tax-related ones. It was helpful to watch the instructor put the figures on a board. The downside to videos is that they cannot be watched while you are driving, or at least it's not advisable.

- **Continuing education courses** – If you hold certain licenses connected to your profession you may have to take a required amount of CE credits each year to keep that license. There is a tendency to look upon these as simply a requirement and many times easy courses are chosen to simply meet the requirement. Look upon these courses as opportunities to gain knowledge that will help you with your profession and clients. Choose courses that are meaningful for the advancement of your career.

• **Designation studies** – I have a few designations indicated by letters following my name. All of these courses taught me to be better at my job. Your profession may offer courses that will improve your effectiveness. Additionally, public recognition of these designations makes clients view you as a person with expertise. To determine which ones are best for you, ask others in your industry what they have found to be the most valuable.

You probably have company training courses you can take that also further your career. If you acquire the right kind of knowledge, you will be more effective. Just don't become a member of the Flat Earth Society!

TIME ALLOCATION

If misappropriation of time were a crime, most of us would need to worry about being arrested. In my case, there might even be enough evidence to convict me.

When I speak of misappropriation of time I'm not just talking about goofing off. It is possible to misappropriate your time to an excessive work schedule. Individuals who do this are called "workaholics." In my youth, I was extremely guilty of this syndrome. There were many holidays on which I could be found sitting behind my desk at the office. I ended up with ulcers and faltered relationships. I'm a little better at choosing how I allocate my time today, but I still need an occasional reminder to keep things in perspective.

By now, you have probably noticed that I use the phrase "time allocation" instead of "time management." I have never had much success in managing time. When I set out to manage time, it shows me who is boss. I can arrive at the office with my day planned out and have my whole day changed by my first phone call from a client, a surprise audit from the SEC (this has happened), or a new mandate from corporate superiors. In those instances, I have been unable to manage "time." I can try to allocate my time, but I cannot control it.

The first step in determining how to allocate one's time is to decide what is important. What results do you want to achieve? Items of importance also need to be categorized and ranked. Which item is more important than another? Once the prioritization is completed, time segments can be appropriately allocated. Let me illustrate questionable ranking of topics by using an example.

Many years ago I was invited to a meeting of the Junior Chamber of Commerce (Jaycees). After the group finished its normal business updates, the reading of the minutes, and introductions of new members and attendees, discussions were opened for debate to determine how specific issues would be resolved.

The first item introduced for discussion was storage of the group's popcorn machine. The machine was placed at local events and was a fundraiser for the Jaycees. Between events, the machine needed to be placed in storage. But, where would that location be? I was amazed at how long this debate lasted. It took more than forty minutes to decide to place it in a storage closet. The closet was located in a building already used by the group to store other items.

The next item discussed was who would be awarded a $5,000 scholarship. This meeting was more than forty years ago so an equivalent inflation-adjusted number today would probably be around $25,000. There were three contenders for this award. Some of the Jaycee members had never heard of any of the three candidates.

Less than five minutes later, the decision had been made. One name would receive the funds. It took more than forty minutes to determine where to store a popcorn machine, but less than five minutes to award a big scholarship. I could not help but wonder if the time involved in the decisions that night had been properly allocated.

Before I discuss corporate meetings I should give a little background about me. I was raised on a farm in western Kansas. We were a small farm so all of the family members needed to participate in farm activities. Some family members fed chickens and gathered their eggs. Some slopped the pigs. A couple of us milked the dairy cattle. Anyone able to drive a tractor or combine was occasionally called upon to do so. All tasks were shared or delegated.

Since everyone had a working knowledge of the farm operations, each one of us was permitted to voice our opinions. This was done at our daily meeting, which occurred at the kitchen dining table each evening. My dad believed in "participatory management" long before I had even heard of the term. He wanted our input and we gave it. We collectively made decisions around that table: which crops would be planted and where, how would we eliminate the weeds encroaching on our crops, when to begin harvesting a crop, etc. Very little time was wasted at dinner. We planned business operations while eating. We still had fun with the family, though. It wasn't all about business. We also used this time to catch up on what was happening in each family member's life.

Like my first meeting with the Jaycees, I have often felt that some time is wasted in corporate meetings. I've noticed that some managers seem to schedule regular meetings even when those meetings might not be needed. I suspect that some of these meetings are conducted with all department employees so one or two of them can be monitored. It is a simple truth that some employees require more attention than others.

Some employees need to be closely managed to make sure that they are being productive. It is necessary to have those employees report on their weekly progress on projects. However, if the department has seven productive members and one who is less productive, is it efficient to have each department member recite what he or she is doing? This ties up the time of all the department members and probably reduces overall department productivity. Wouldn't an individual meeting with the less productive employee be more efficient and productive?

I remember sitting through several meetings at a small organization I worked for many years ago. It seemed like the main purpose of those meetings was to schedule the next meeting. Very little was actually accomplished in those sessions. I remember stating that the company spent so much time talking about what it was going to do that no one had time to actually do anything. I added that it would be hard for the company to continue to exist if it kept following this procedure. (The company no longer exists. It was acquired years ago by another entity).

I have to admit that there are times when a manager will knowingly waste a department's time in a meeting. I have personally experienced this situation. Because the corporation I worked for was not ready to release information that a product line was being eliminated, I had to conduct meetings as though the product would be continued. This was a necessary misappropriation of time that was unavoidable.

A sidebar to these observations is that some managers push for projects that are not conducive to revenue generation or expense reduction. I have had managers insist that I produce an item that I knew would never be used. The manager was adamant that the item be created, so I followed orders and produced it. The item was never used. In one instance only three items were ordered by a sales force consisting of forty thousand. Was this a proper allocation of corporate assets? If you are a corporate manager, you need to evaluate how effective a project might be. Sometimes it is necessary to try something to see if it will work, but I have had managers insist we try a procedure that had failed five times already at the same company. You do not need to create nonproductive busy work to justify your existence.

In a discussion after one of my speeches, a financial advisor told me that he had finally succeeded in selling an individual the life insurance the individual needed for his family. He stated that it took twenty appointments to make the sale. I suspect that the policyholder bought the policy simply to get rid of the agent. This agent was extremely proud that he had made life insurance funds available for the client's family. I complimented him on his persistence, but asked him if he felt he had allocated his time properly.

On the one hand, he had helped a family secure the life insurance coverage that was badly needed. On the other hand, there might be twenty other families that do not have the coverage needed because he spent so much time with this client. Since we cannot predict the future (unless we have prophetic abilities) I cannot say this advisor made the wrong choice. He might have made the right one. But, he should at least evaluate how he is allocating his time. Was he concerned about the breadwinner in this case, or was he simply reluctant to pursue another prospect?

I mentioned earlier that one needs to prioritize what is important to him or her. The ranking chosen ultimately affects the end results of one's activities. For example, I know an individual who focused on producing a lot of money as a consultant. He achieved his desired result and made a lot of money. To do that, he spent several years traveling around the country to serve the needs of high net-worth clients. He was always on the road. Rarely was he home with his wife and family. When he was with them, and his cell phone rang, he always took the call. (I don't know how you feel, but if I am with someone and they answer the phone in the middle of our conversation, I assume that I am not very important to that individual). His family made the same assumption. Today, he does not understand why his children spend very little time with him. Maybe it is because when they were children, he did not spend much time with them.

Like all of us, most people have a goal - a dream. There is something they hope to accomplish. I admire people that have these goals and aggressively pursue them, but when selecting a dream a person needs to really evaluate what is important to him or her. I have met people who have accomplished their dream only to find out that their dream wasn't what they thought it would be once they got there.

Years ago, I met a lady who owned a small book store. I love reading books so much that the thought of owning a book store even occurred to me in my youth. I asked her how she came to own the store.

"I've always loved reading," she said. "I love books so much that I decided to buy a book store so I could be around them all the time. But, after owning the store for a couple of years I am less attracted to books. I have to inventory all the books, place orders for them, pay sales taxes on those sold, keep the accounting records for the store, etc. In fact, the store keeps me so busy that I no longer have time to read. When I get home, I am so tired I usually fall asleep while watching the news. I don't even get weekends off, because my store is open. I dreamed of owning the store. Now, I wish I could sell it." When she achieved her dream it was not what she thought it would be.

I heard a world famous athlete talk about achieving her dream. She had won an Olympic gold medal. Can you imagine the hours she worked to achieve her dream? Winning the gold medal gave her fame and money. However, shortly thereafter, she realized that the gold medal had not given her happiness. In fact, she was under a great deal of pressure to compete again to try to get another gold medal.

After self-analysis she realized what was important. It wasn't the gold medal. The stress of competing again was affecting her health, her relationships, and more. She decided she would not try to get another gold medal and retired. Today, after realizing what is important to her, she smiles a lot more.

You need to evaluate how you allocate your time. You want to avoid improper allocation. If your health is important to you, you need to make time for exercise and entertainment. If you want to maintain great relationships with your spouse, children, and friends, time must be allocated to them. Put balance in your life and your stress levels will improve. With proper allocation of your time, you'll need fewer medications to cope with life. Remember, you must allocate time to your business, your family, and your friends, but even more importantly, you need to allocate time to you.

WHO'S THE DECISION MAKER?

We do not need an alarm clock in our house. At 5:15 AM a little gray miniature Schnauzer barks a couple of times to announce that it is time for us to arise. If we ignore him, he moves to the next level of communication. He makes a noise that sounds like a screeching eagle diving for its prey. If it only lasted a few seconds we could roll over and go back to sleep. But, he is persistent. He climbs up on one of us, looks in our face and continues the screeching eagle imitation. He "decides" that it is time for us to awaken. It is a decision with which we must comply or possibly go deaf.

About five times each day our Tabby cat finds us and communicates his desire to be held or fed. The sound he makes is similar to the siren on a European ambulance on its way to an accident. We have no choice. We must reckon with the sound. Failure to do so guarantees a rise in our blood pressure. We must comply with his command. The Tabby "decides" what we should do, and when. We have tried to resist his commands, but that leads to a continuation of the decibels he is generating. All we have to do to make the sound cease is give in to his demands.

At about 5:40 AM our Scottie dog (Beam Me Up) heads for the front door. He barks to let us know it is time for his daily walk. If we don't respond quickly enough he approaches us and provides a reminder "nip" at our knees. He has "decided" that it is time for us to comply with his request. Once we hook his harness up, he calms down and puts his nose to the front door in anticipation of the trip. It's a simple step to eliminate the barking and the nipping – all we need to do is take him for his walk.

In each of these scenarios, you can easily determine who the decision makers are. When we have visitors that stay overnight they quickly recognize that my wife and I are not the decision makers in these circumstances. We are the ones that carry out the decisions.

Determining who the decision maker is greatly increases one's success in any situation. Even children quickly figure out which parent is easiest to approach for approval of a request. Mom might say "no" but Dad will usually give his approval. So, they ask Dad.

In the business arena it is not always as easy to recognize who the actual decision maker is. Just because an individual holds a title does not mean he or she can decide to approve a project. Sometimes, even the owner of the business is not the one that will make a final decision. This is often true for financial decisions.

When I was a child I watched a successful life insurance agent sit at our kitchen table and make a presentation to my father and mother. I was too young to understand what he was talking about, but it was easy for me to tell that he acted as though my mother was not even in the room. The entire presentation was directed to my dad. After the presentation was over, my father looked at my mother and then at the agent and said he would think about the proposal and contact the agent later. I knew the agent was never going to make a sale to anyone in our family.

What the agent did not know was that my father was a genius at farming and mechanical endeavors. But, my dad did not like to keep the accounting records for the farm, nor did he like to make many of the financial decisions. Mom handled all of the family and farm finances, and the agent had totally ignored her. She was offended by the way the agent had treated her. She was never going to buy anything from him. In this case, she was the decision maker, and she had been ignored. When my mom died, my father was lost with regard to the farm finances. He did not know where any of the important papers were located. Eventually, he hired a farm management company to handle the business accounting.

What I found interesting is that twenty year later I went on a sales call with another life insurance agent and experienced a similar scenario. The farm couple was in their upper forties. Because I was young and new to the financial services industry, I was just to observe and learn from the agent. He did the same thing as the man who tried to sell my parents life insurance. He made the entire presentation to the husband. He barely acknowledged the wife's presence. If the wife asked a question, he gave the answer to the husband. After the presentation he made several attempts to close the sale, but was unsuccessful. He acted like my presence had interfered with his sale. But, I do not think he would have made the sale, even if I had not been there. I believe the wife was the decision maker in this scenario, and she felt slighted, just like my mom had.

I suspect that many sales or new ideas fail to happen because the product or idea is "pitched" to someone who cannot make the decision to proceed. Making a determination of who can authorize the process to move forward solely by observation can be difficult. More analysis of the situation is necessary. Whether you are pitching a new department procedure to your boss, a new product for your company to manufacture, or a solution to one of your clients, convincing someone to implement your idea will have greater success if you are trying to persuade the decision maker. Otherwise, you are probably wasting your time and that of the other individual.

Decision makers come in many roles. The decision-making capacity varies with the individuals you meet. Sometimes there are layers to overcome to reach the decision maker. The first decision maker might be the receptionist. He or she screens off many people every day by determining who gets to see the boss. Screenings might include phone calls in which the caller is told the boss is not in, while the boss sits in the office working on projects. It might be necessary to develop a relationship with the receptionist first. If the receptionist also screens incoming mail, a letter or sales brochure might not have a great deal of success getting to the boss either. Some of the companies I previously worked with recognized the importance of the receptionist. Attempts were made to build important friendships with these receptionists. My company would send small gifts to them (candy, event tickets, etc.). Occasionally, we talked to the receptionist about how our product or service might help his or her boss be more productive and how we might reduce his or her stress level. What receptionist doesn't want a happier boss?

If you sell cars, you probably know the importance of involving the wife in a selection process. We men are very attracted to shiny sports cars or big pickup trucks. The wife helps to remind us that we need a vehicle that can hold seven people, including the five children. She also thinks about the old washer that's about to die, and wants to keep some money available for that occurrence. The best decision will be a joint decision, so input from both partners is needed.

Some people who have a title that makes them appear to be a decision maker do not like making decisions. In my career I have encountered managers like this. Sometimes this is a good thing. Managers do not always have the knowledge needed to make the right decision. An employee or two might know what decision should be made. Therefore, it becomes necessary for the manager to ask for input. Even Star Trek captains ask for input. But, once the facts are in, someone has to make the decision. It can be a committee, if necessary, but no forward progress will be made until a decision is made. If you are trying to get a decision made, you will need to learn to recognize the decision making process.

You cannot assume that the owner or president of the company is the decision maker for the product or idea you are promoting. As a company becomes larger, some decisions are delegated to other people. Do you think the president of a large corporation determines what paper is used in the printers? Of course not, he or she is too busy. Even the big decisions (e.g., mergers, development of new products, moving the office, etc.) may involve a committee or the CFO. Very large companies may require stockholders to vote their shares to decide what should be done. You will need to determine the decision making process for any organization with which you are working to have greater success building a mutual relationship with it.

If you have worked with government agencies you know that almost all decisions involve a committee. You should ask about this process early in your conversations. It will still take many weeks (or months) for the decision to occur, but finding out what the steps are could shorten the time involved.

A few years ago, I worked with an advisor who had spent many weeks talking to a government organization about positioning some of its assets in various investments he sold. I asked him if he checked on the process involved. He told me he had been told that there was a committee involved. I suggested he talk to some of the committee members before he proceeded further. He discovered that the bylaws of the organization only permitted investments in local bond issues, which he did not offer. He had wasted a lot of time on a prospect that could not buy anything he offered. He should have talked to the decision makers earlier.

If you ever study business management courses, you will learn about a company's organizational chart. It's easy to analyze a company's organizational chart. The chart lists the employee titles and positions in the organization from top to bottom. One look at the chart and you might deduce who you should see about making a decision. Unfortunately, it is not that simple. Your assessment might be wrong.

Within any organization is an "informal organization." You cannot find a chart for the informal organization. It is not printed anywhere. It is an invisible structure that exists in any organization that has more than one person. If you observe an organization's operations you will begin to see the informal structure. For example, you will notice that employees do not always go to the department head for an answer. They take their questions to the one that has the answer. These mentors often make decisions affecting the business operations, even though the organization's chart grants the authority to someone else. If you analyze your own company, you will probably begin to see the informal organization that exists in it. Recognizing the informal structure might help you get decisions made more rapidly.

So, if you are trying to motivate a company or individual to take an action you have proposed, how do you decide who will make the decision for you? Perhaps these observations will be helpful.

If you are making a presentation to two partners, do not make any assumptions about who the decision maker is. Make your presentation to both of them. Make eye contact with each one. Involve both of them. The quiet one might be the one who will decide to take up your project or buy your product. As you make your presentation watch for clues from body languages, or from questions that are being asked. Notice if one partner defers to the other. Often, by the end of your presentation you may know who has the capacity to choose to move forward.

Sometimes you can ask other people who have worked with the business. They can often provide insight regarding which individual(s) to approach. They might tell you that Frank is the one who makes decisions about how to manage the customers and employees. But, Joe is the one who will authorize the business to move forward with your proposal. Knowing how to approach the business managers before you make the presentation might increase your odds for success.

From most of my chapters in this book you have probably noticed that I am a big advocate of asking questions. I have even found that I can often locate the decision maker by simply asking who it is. My question might be, "Mr./Ms. Prospect, if we decide that by choosing my product (or idea) your business gains a valuable commodity, can you describe the process which your company undertakes to decide to purchase my product or service (implement the idea)? Are you the one who decides to move ahead? Or, is there a committee I need to meet with?"

Most of the time, people are happy to provide answers to my questions. In fact, I often I get a detailed explanation of the purchase order process. The answers usually explain how the action will be implemented. I believe that you will find this to be true for you, as well. If you ask for an explanation of the implementation process, you will be told the steps involved. Once you know who makes the decision regarding your proposal, and how it will be implemented, you won't waste time talking to the wrong individuals. Time is valuable to you and the person you are seeing. Learn to respect it.

COMPETITION

About fifteen miles from where I grew up was an oval race track. On Sunday nights they had jalopy races. I used to enjoy going with a half dozen of my friends. One night while watching the races, one of my friends said, "We ought to race jalopies. If we all went together we could buy an old car to race. Some of us are good mechanics, and I'm a good driver. All we need to do is place third or higher and we will make enough prize money to keep us going." Jalopy racing in that little town was not an expensive sport at that time. Entry fees were low and old cars were cheap.

The idea was too tempting. We all agreed and got a couple more friends to join with us. The thought of being part of the pit crew inside the oval track was irresistible. Each of us pooled our money, and the driver found a car he thought would do well.

The experience was amazing. We didn't have the fastest car, but we had one of the most talented drivers on the track. Many a time we saw him reach the curve positioned in the middle of the jalopy pack and emerge at the end of the curve in one of the top three places. He did this so often we almost expected him to place every time. All winnings were reinvested into car maintenance and track fees. It was a fun way to spend our Sunday evenings.

We liked winning, but we did not get upset if we did not win. Our sole purpose in racing our jalopy was to have fun. We really did not view the other drivers as competitors. They were simply participants in the game. We knew that our driver was excellent, and he enabled us to keep enjoying our participation in the sport. We were not trying to make a lot of money. We were just trying to have fun.

Business ventures are different. We want our products to compete. We need to make a certain amount of income to enjoy the lifestyle we desire. We all know that our products need to be reasonably competitive to sell well. If we are selling the same car models as the dealership a mile away and our cars are priced twice as high we know our customers will simply drive a few more blocks to get the better deal. Price plays an initial factor in a customer's product selection.

If we are selling a product that has low quality (it is known to break down often) our product will be more difficult to sell. If we have a restaurant and the news reports that our food makes people sick, our customers will go to a competitor. Product quality is another factor affecting a customer's buying decision. We all know these things about competition in the business world. However, if our product is close in price and quality, and our company is respected for its integrity and service, the dynamic of the business changes. Our business's success will depend on its relationships with its customers.

You already know the importance of your relationships in your personal product selections. Some of you regularly see the same hair stylist, not because he or she is the cheapest in town, but because you know that you will receive a good haircut. I choose my stylist because she can cut my hair without making me look too bald – an important factor at my age. If she is on maternity leave I may use another stylist, but as soon as she returns I am willing to stand in line waiting for her skills to make me look beautiful. Okay, that's a stretch, but you know what I mean.

If I have a problem with my car and the problem is not covered under the dealer warranty, I take the machine to my favorite mechanic. He isn't cheaper than anyone else, but he is good. I know he will fix my problem and that he will stand behind his work. Because I am a loyal customer he always gets me in, even when he is extremely busy. That's worth a lot to me.

I hire a company to provide lawn service for me. They do not mow my grass, but they apply all the appropriate chemicals to foster growth and eliminate weeds. Before hiring the company I use now, I used a nationally recognized company, but I was never really pleased with the way I was treated. It seemed like each time someone came to service my yard, it was a different person than the last time they were there. Now, I use a small company located in a suburb of the town where I reside. He calls me by name when he shows up. He works hard to make me happy. When he is done he closes all the gates so my dogs won't get out. His prices are about the same as every other lawn service company, but that is not the most important issue.

What's important to me is the relationship I have with him. I know he is going to treat me and my yard right.

I also have a similar relationship with my bank. The branch manager where I conduct most of my business is named Matthew. If he is there when I go into the bank, he always says, "Hi, Steve," unless he is with a customer. When my wife goes to the bank, he says, "Hi, Juliann. How's work?" This may seem like a trivial matter, but I grew up in a very small community in western Kansas and that's what it was like back there. When I went to the local bank, I was always greeted by name. Matthew gives me that feeling again, even though he is part of a large local bank network. The bank's fees are similar to every other bank in town – it's the relationship I have with the bank manager that keeps me going there.

Relationships with customers depend on our actions. When customers know we are trustworthy, they are more likely to conduct their business with us. And, they will continue to do business with us. They want to know that we will stand behind our product or service. (If we put a new roof on their house but it still leaks, they need to know we will fix it.) They let their friends know we are reliable. If we say we are going to do something, and then we do it, our reputation is enhanced and fosters good relationships. When we treat our customers with respect, they come back. So, how is a good relationship developed with your clients?

If you want to keep a competitor from taking over a client, you must be the best source of the products or services you offer. If you are his or her best source for the types of products he wants or needs, or the best service he can get, the client is less likely to look elsewhere for assistance. Even when he or she is approached by a competitor, your client will tell the competitor he is already happy with your company. I have had that happen to me. I have called a potential prospect and was told that they are happy with their advisor. I appreciate and respect those relationships. In fact, I hope my clients say the same thing when my competitors call them.

You are responsible for some of the work in maintaining your client relationships. You need to help your client remember that he or she has a relationship with you. You do this by your actions. Let me show one simple way that I did this for my clients. It did not take much effort, but it did help solidify my client relations. The little extra effort I put into serving my clients helped keep competitors at bay. I take these extra steps to make future planning sessions easier and to give my client ready access to the information I have provided. In those situations where my product is similar to those being offered by other advisors, a stronger relationship with my client preserves the business.

If you have read other chapters in this book, you should know by now how I create a financial plan for my client. It's a two-step process. My first step is acquisition of client information. In other words, step one is fact-finding. After gathering the facts so I can build a solution to help the client meet his or her needs, I meet with the client and go over my recommendations. I offer a variety of products from which they can choose. From my recommendations, my clients select the products they feel most comfortable with. Then, we complete the appropriate applications.

When I return to deliver the client's products that have been selected by them, I provide them with a thick notebook. The notebook contains a copy of the financial plan, important documents (wills, guardianships, etc.), product brochures, and more. Also included are copies of applications for mutual funds and accompanying prospectuses, life insurance policies, and anything else that was relevant. I also include all of their products, even if the product was purchased from another advisor or broker. I explain to the client that keeping all of their information together makes it easier to monitor how their plan is working in future analyses. Also, I label the products to reflect the reason they were purchased.

For example, if I sold an investment that was to provide college funds for their child, Timmy, I put that product in the notebook with a label that said, "This investment is for Timmy's college." If they look at the notebook later with a competitor, they will remember that the investment is for Timmy's education. The emotions that are stirred in them make it more difficult for a competitor to replace the product. In fact, it is rare for them to even talk to a competitor.

Sometimes financial advisors worry too much about competition. Many times competition is not a factor in their relationship with their clients. I remember the uproar that occurred when insurance companies started letting banks sell annuities. Insurance representatives were irate over this. They forgot that they were in a relationship business, and that most of them would not be affected greatly by banks selling these products. In fact, I told many of them that their annuity sales might increase. They were now offering a product that banks offered. What an endorsement that would be for the products the insurance rep offered. Suddenly, more credibility was given to annuity products.

Many of the sales reps I talked to also held securities licenses. I reminded them that every securities broker in their town offered American Funds (mutual funds) as an investment choice. Most of the reps I talked to offered these funds as well. So, if every broker in town offers the same mutual funds you do, and it has not affected your client relations or sales success, why would you think banks selling annuities will? Eventually, the insurance reps discovered that their annuity sales were not negatively impacted by annuity sales in banks. In fact, their sales of annuities may have been enhanced. The relationship with their client was still intact.

Instead of worrying about the product mix you offer your clients, focus on the relationship. If your relationship is strong, it will be difficult for a competitor to work with your client. It's like a good marriage. When a couple's marriage is strong, it is difficult for another suitor to become involved with either spouse.

Now, I am not going to tell you that you will never lose a client to a competitor. That happens. I have had it happen to me. Some situations were really beyond my control. For example, the client's son entered the business and wanted Mom to purchase her investments or insurance from him. In some instances when the son was no longer in the business, the client looked me up to be his advisor again. I was able to get the client back. Remember, the odds of losing a client to a competitor are greatly reduced when your client relationship is strong.

Although this is a short article, my point is clear. Concentrate on the relationship you have with your client. Provide the best service you can. Be friendly, be reliable, be trustworthy, display integrity, and provide the expertise they may not be able to locate elsewhere. Let them see that your objective is to serve their need and you will have a continuing relationship with them. The stronger your client relationships, the less likely a competitor can penetrate your domain. Competition is not really an issue when a good relationship exists.

REFERRALS

During my junior year of college my roommate, Don, got married. A year later, he called and said he needed my help. He wanted to know if I knew an honest life insurance agent. His wife was pregnant, and he was concerned about providing for her and the baby if something happened to him. Don and his wife did not have a lot of money, so they needed to purchase insurance that did not cost too much. He was still in college and had a few months to go before he would graduate.

Don was studying to be an engineer, so it was a good bet that he would get a good job after graduating. However, in the meantime he wanted financial assurance for his family. I was impressed with how responsible he had become in only a few months. When I was his roommate he displayed a "party" mentality. I told Don I would introduce him and his wife to an agent with the highest integrity.

We arranged a time for them to meet the agent, Ben. I, too, met with them and Ben at Don's apartment. After I introduced them to each other, Don asked me to stay for the presentation. I think he felt that my presence would help assure that Ben would treat them right.

I listened to Ben's presentation. Because of Don's income limitations at the time, the agent gave Don a few term insurance premium rates. (These were the days of rate books, so it took a little longer to manually calculate the premium amounts). Also, since this was a time before computers had been invented, Ben could not produce a printout. However, the insurance company provided a colorful brochure that Ben could write the premium numbers on. After Ben's presentation, Don and Ben completed the insurance application for the amount Don could afford, and Don wrote a check for the first premium.

When they were done, Ben thanked Don and his wife for the business. Ben did not make a lot of money on the term insurance sale, but he made sure Don's wife would have available funds if something happened to Don. Then, Ben lifted the application to write on it and said, "Now, Don, I need to get a couple of names from you as credit references. These should be people that are employed. It's just something the company requires." Don provided names of a couple of their friends.

When we left I asked Ben, "Does your company really ask you to get names as credit references for such a small policy?"

"No, replied Ben. The company has two blanks on the application to get the names, but they are used as leads. We are to call the people named to see if they have an insurance need and try to set up an appointment."

I pondered what he had just said. "But you don't know anything about the names Don provided. What if they can't qualify for the insurance because they are in poor health? What if they can't pay the premiums? What if Don could have given you more names, or more qualified names?"

Ben looked at me and answered, "It's just an easy way to get names from a client. They don't feel reluctant to give me names when they think they are just providing credit references. Most people are hesitant to give their friends' names to an insurance agent. Most people simply do not want to talk to a life insurance agent."

"But, Ben, you are going to have to do detective work now. You have to call the names, try to meet with them, and try to convince them to buy insurance. They might not even have a need for life insurance at this time. Most of Don's friends are going to be unemployed or low-paid college students. That sure seems like an inefficient approach to locate prospective clients." I waited for his response.

He replied, "I do have to investigate the people a little more, but at least it gives me a couple of people to call. Once they become clients I am able to ask them for referrals to their friends or family members using the same approach. There may be better ways to get referrals, but this is one the company suggests we use. It works. I get names from the applicants and follow up with phone calls."

Don had given Ben a couple of names, and Ben was happy to get them. But, they really weren't referrals. Don never gave Ben any other information about the names he provided. All the work to determine if Ben provided a product these names could use was up to Ben. A qualified referred lead can be an excellent source of new business to a salesman. But, a qualified referred lead is more than just a name. If you have enough information about the person named, a qualified lead can be the best lead you receive. Let's review the importance of a qualified referral.

Have you ever asked a friend for the name of a good plumber, accountant, mechanic, barber, or electrician? Perhaps you never needed one before. Or, maybe the one you chose personally did a poor job for you. You asked your friend, because you knew your friend would give you the name of someone reliable and qualified to do the work you needed done, if your friend knew someone. Also, you were pretty sure the name provided by your friend would provide service to you at an affordable rate.

Let's assume you are at a backyard barbecue with several of your friends. On the way to the party, your car started making strange noises. It's obvious that you need to find a good mechanic. As you visit with your friends you mention that your car is making strange noises. You ask if one of them knows a good mechanic. A couple of friends provide the name of a mechanic they both use. They bubble over with comments about how great this mechanic is. The next day you call the mechanic they suggested. Prior to the party you had never heard of him. Your friends' referral was all you needed. You trust them and followed through on their recommendations. A couple of days later, you have a car that runs properly.

I have often asked my friends and clients for a referral to a good accountant, a professional plumber, or an electrician. Besides being able to give me the name of a good one, they can steer me away from the bad ones. The referral helps me make decisions about the service professional I will use.

For any of us in business, the referral is an important aid in helping us find new clients. But, just getting a name to contact is not enough. When we ask for a referral, we should specify what types of individuals or businesses we seek. We should let the referrer know the parameters we want (e.g., prospect's age, marital status, income level, residence location, business type, etc.). The client may have to work a little harder to come up with names that fit with our referral parameters but narrowing our referral parameters will give us better names to contact. The names we get will be people who could qualify to buy our product and who might also want our product.

If you sell Chevrolets and the person you are talking to has never owned anything but Fords for more than forty years, he or she probably is not a good candidate for one of your Chevys. When asking for a referral, you need to ask for names of people that want to own a Chevrolet.

If you paint houses, and the person you plan to contact lives in a house covered in vinyl siding, he or she may not find your paint products enticing. So, when requesting a referred lead, you should ask for names of people that live in wood residences. Perhaps your client knows someone whose house needs painting.

If you own a computer dating service, your business will probably not be appealing to a happily married person. When you ask for a referral, you would tell your client you need people who are single and interested in getting married.

If you are in the financial services arena, you want referrals that can use your products. You will need to define the type of referral you need. He or she should be someone that fits your skill level. The referral should be someone that needs a product you sell. For example, if you do not sell Medicare supplement programs you would not seek individuals that need this type of insurance.

You can purchase sales materials that help you ask clients for referrals. Even when I started in the life insurance business the "You'll Earn a Fortune" sales materials had a section to ask for referred leads. It was a colorful flip chart that went through the various activities to which your client might belong. The flip chart was used to jog the client's memory. It asked the client about people they knew at work, in their neighborhood, their family, their church associates, their social club friends, and the like. The flip chart then helped explain what types of products you offered. It was an easy sales script and produced many qualified referrals. At the time my company emphasized that we get at least two names for follow up. It seems this was a common practice in the industry.

One night, at a regional meeting of insurance sales reps, we were sitting around a table at the hotel comparing sales techniques. One of the sales reps at the table regularly sold two hundred policies each year. Naturally, we all wanted to know how he found his prospects. The first thing he said was that he usually got eight to ten referrals from each client. No one had ever told him to only get two names. The device he used was fairly simple. He told us he had created it himself, and we were surprised by its simplicity. He pulled a copy from his notebook (not a computer, an actual notebook) and showed us what he used.

His form was two-sided. Both sides had a circle drawn in the upper one-third of the paper. He had hand-produced the form himself. It did not have glossy pages or colorful photographs. It was just simple printer paper and the circles were hand drawn. On one side of the paper was a circle divided like one might cut a pie (a pie chart). Each section of the pie chart listed groups in which the client might be a member. The sections contained titles like: Employment, PTA, Church, lodges, country clubs, social clubs, family, and the like. The circle on the back side was also divided like a pie and listed the services the producer provided: health insurance, disability insurance life insurance, investments, long term care insurance, etc. The front side of the form also had ten lines under the pie chart for names and phone numbers.

When the agent was done with his presentation he would pull the form out and set it in front of the client. "Mr./Ms. Client," he would say, "Now that I have helped you solve a problem, I need your help. Some of your friends probably have similar problems. I know if we were at a party or church meeting you would introduce me to them. That's kind of what I am asking for now - an introduction. If you could provide the names of some of your acquaintances and friends, I will happily follow up with them to try to ease their financial burdens." Then he would explain that the form showed the services he provided on one side and contained groups they might belong to on the other side. He said he always got at least eight names and numbers.

One of the agents in the room, Dan, asked if he could have a copy of the form. Dan took the form back to his office and made photocopies. Then, he used it at his next client meeting. He called me a week later. "Steve, do you remember the 'referred lead' form that was discussed last week at the hotel? You won't believe it. It really works. I put the form in front of my client, gave the little speech, and waited for the client to start filling in names. He gave me ten names. I've never had that many referrals before. If I have this kind of luck every time, I'll never run out of prospects."

I have met financial advisors that get their clients to write a short note on the advisor's brochure. The note from the client suggests that the friend meet with the advisor to discuss his or her financial objectives. The note also mentions that the advisor has helped them with their plans. The advisor takes the brochure back to his or her office and mails it to the name the client provided. A few days later the advisor follows up with a call to set up an appointment. What prospect can refuse to talk to a sales rep that their friend has just recommended? Very few can, because they do not want to offend their friend.

A center-of-influence (COI) is an extremely valuable asset for any business. The COI can also be priceless for a financial advisor. A COI sends you clients, or gives you the names of potential clients. Let me give you an example.

When I moved to Iowa I contacted a realtor to help me find a house to replace the one I had sold in Kansas City. After looking at several, we made an offer on the one in which we currently reside. The realtor we used worked with lenders every day and knew which ones were easiest to work with and which ones had the best mortgage terms. The realtor arranged for us to meet with a lender and even accompanied us to the meeting. It was obvious to us that the realtor and the lender had worked together before. They had a close relationship. The mortgage process turned out to be easy. Within a few minutes we were completing the mortgage application. Then, the realtor asked us if we knew a property casualty agent. We already had one, but if we did not have one, he could have made a connection to one. This, of course, helped the realtor complete his sale, but it also helped the lender, and in some cases, the PC agent. The realtor was a COI for the lender and the PC agent.

Some car dealers have similar arrangements with lenders and auto insurance agents. If you are buying a car they can help you find a lender. Also, if you do not have an auto insurance agent they can make the introduction to one. The car dealer is a COI for the lender and agent.

Some financial advisors have excellent luck with third-party centers-of-influence, too. They build relationships with accountants and attorneys who send clients to the advisor. For example, an estate planning attorney might send a client to the financial advisor to purchase a life insurance policy that is needed to cover estate taxes when the client dies. Or, an accountant might send a client to the advisor because the client needs a tax deduction. Perhaps a qualified plan for the small business would help provide an immediate tax deduction. Maybe an IRA would be the right product for an individual. I have had several advisors tell me they have had successes like this. So, I think it is a good idea for you to try to develop COI relationships like these.

I wish that I could tell you that I have had an excellent track record with COIs, but, alas, I cannot. After trying to develop COI relationships, I finally asked some of them why they were reluctant to send their clients to me. They explained that it was not because they did not have faith in my skills. They further added that it was not because they were afraid of exposing themselves to a legal claim if they referred someone to me. They told me that their reluctance was based on their desire to protect their own sources of referrals.

One estate planning attorney told me that he acquired clients from several life insurance producers in town. "If I send a client to you and the other agents find out about it, how many new prospects do you think they will send to me?" An accountant basically told me the same thing. I learned that I can certainly let them know that I am available to help their clients, but I cannot expect them to risk their relationships with other financial advisors in the community. If you are in a small community where there are fewer advisors with the same expertise you possess, you might have better success getting referrals from COIs. Or, if your uncle is one of the COIs, you might have more success. The point I am making is this: Don't be afraid to try to develop the COI, but if it doesn't happen, use the other referred lead techniques available to you.

Another source of referred leads is leads you purchase. There are organizations that will sell you referred leads. My success purchasing referred leads is mixed. I've had both good success and horrible results. Some of these organizations furnish excellent leads. They have been sorted and selected to meet my parameters for the lead. They match with the products and services I provide.

Other providers of referred leads simply provide names. I have often arrived at an appointment that came from one of these referred lead marketers only to discover that the lead was not a fit for my products or services. In some cases the individual or company could not qualify for my products. Unfortunately, when the lead was not a good fit, I had incurred an expense without a revenue result. The only way I was able to find out which referral companies provided good referred leads was to try them. Of course, another effective way to find a good company selling referred leads is to get your company or another advisor to refer you to one.

I must admit that many of my best clients have come from a referral. If their friend who provided me the referral also told them about me before I arrived, the referral usually knew how I worked and what to expect. In those instances I encountered less resistance. The lead was more receptive to my ideas. These individuals readily answered questions during the fact-finding process. I highly recommend that you ask for referred leads in every client meeting. Just don't limit yourself to two, and get your client to tell you a little history about the referral. You will be better positioned to help them. A satisfied client keeps referrals flowing.

SEMINAR SELLING

Early in my career I discovered the value of seminar selling. There wasn't much seminar competition back then. Because most financial advisors did not offer seminars, I was able to get good attendance to my programs. Attendees did not have a lot of alternative seminars that they could attend. Today, so many financial planners use seminars that it is much more difficult to get a good turnout. Also, producing a seminar is more costly. Competition has caused a rise in costs.

When your competitor offers a fancy meal to attract attendees, you are forced to as well. Of course, there is a cost for the meals you provide. Also, restaurants often charge a fee for you to rent the room where the seminar will be conducted. There are also costs for mailing the invitations. Total costs to hold a seminar can easily cost $5,000, so you need to make sure you get qualified prospects in the room to hear your presentation. Your goal is to acquire new clients, so you should invite attendees that are a good fit for what you offer.

Don't get me wrong. I am still an advocate of selling through seminars. The primary advantage of seminar selling is that you can address 50 people at once instead of calling 50 people one at a time on the phone. If your presentation is well-received, and perceived as something offering value, some of the attendees will request follow-up conversations with you. The seminar will have winnowed the crowd down to those who want to know more about the subject matter.

I've had a lot of success with seminars, and over time, I learned a few lessons that made me more effective. I thought it would be beneficial if I pointed out a few of the lessons I've learned. You might check with your company to see if they already have pre-approved seminars you can use. If so, you won't need to develop one and hope the company's compliance department will approve it. Your company might have everything you need (e.g., invitations, follow-up phone scripts, the PowerPoint presentation, and more). Some companies also offer financial assistance with seminar costs. Also, other seminar presenters may be available to provide advice on how to be more effective. I have often found that other seminar presenters are willing to share their experiences with me, and by comparing notes we have helped each other become more effective.

One lesson I acquired from my experiences is that the title of a seminar can greatly affect seminar attendance. Your marketing materials for your seminar must pique a prospect's interest if he or she is to attend. Perhaps this is best illustrated by providing a personal example.

My office was located in a fairly large city. Within a few hours of my office was a prominent lakeside village that was a nationally recognized spot where people often retired. Houses at the lake were expensive, so the people who lived there often owned significant assets. Let me illustrate what these lakeside residents were like. On a trip to that locale, I met a retired janitor worth more than $3,000,000. This was over thirty years ago. Today, an equivalent value of his assets would probably be around $10,000,000. Accumulating that much value was an impressive feat for someone whose income level was average. How did it happen? His career put him in the right place at the right time.

This man had worked at a company that was traded on the New York Stock Exchange. It offered great employee benefits, including a stock purchase plan. Employees could have money withheld from each paycheck to purchase shares in the employer's stock. He signed up for the stock purchase program on his first day of employment. From his very first paycheck the company began purchasing company shares for him.

His employer produced medical supplies that were in high demand, so throughout his employment the company's value grew. By the time he was in his mid-fifties, his shares had grown to a significant sum. He had made the financial sacrifices needed to gain ownership of his shares, and because of his actions, he could see that he would undoubtedly have a good retirement. However, the story, for him, gets even better.

As people often say, lightning struck and he became rich overnight. Because of his employer's success in the medical field, the company became a target for a corporate takeover. Another larger chemical and medical company wanted to add his company's product lines to its product line. The larger chemical company tendered an offer that was very attractive. It offered $53 per share for the stock he and the other stockholders owned. Before the tendered offer, his stock traded around $19 per share. It was too good an offer to refuse, especially since the majority stockholder was at an advanced age and was ready to bow out.

A like-kind exchange was used to complete the purchase transaction. Under this technique, stock of the acquiring company is exchanged for stock of the company being purchased. No cash exchanged hands at that time. Under Section 1031 of the IRS code, the like-kind exchange did not create current income taxation for existing shareholders. Only when the new stock was sold later by the shareholder would a taxable event occur. And, when the stock was eventually sold, it would be treated as a long-term capital gain with favorable tax rates. This was true if only a little stock was sold in each future transaction. When the sale occurred, he received almost three times what his shares were worth before the sale.

Accepting the shares in the new chemical company, a major US company, changed his life. He retired within days of receiving his new shares. He knew he had plenty of money for retirement. All he needed to do was live a life style similar to one he already experienced. He didn't buy one of the most expensive houses in the lakeside community. Owning the fanciest house in the community did not matter to him. The house he bought was a couple of blocks from the lake. But, most importantly, he was retired and was in a place that offered opportunities to play. He could go boating, fishing, swimming, or just watch sunsets while enjoying one of his favorite beverages.

The retired janitor came to my seminar because his new-found wealth gave him estate planning issues. The estate tax exemption at that time was under $1,000,000, so his assets were exposed to a fairly large tax. He was single, so he could not leave the money to a spouse and use a marital exemption to reduce estate taxes. He had nieces and nephews that he was happy to leave his money to, but he was concerned primarily about two things: 1) how much would his estate be impacted by taxes? And, 2) how would his heirs handle the money? I had advertised my estate planning seminar as just that: 1) A seminar addressing ways to address estate planning issues, and, 2) how to protect the assets received by the heirs.

I should mention that estate planning seminars were regularly conducted for residents of this lakeside community. Because the residents were perceived as having money and investments, they were targeted for these types of presentations. In fact, so many seminars like this were produced in the area every month that the residents did not worry about attending one. They reasoned that if they missed one, they could attend the next one. They applied this logic to my seminar and my attendance was not as great as I would have preferred.

My ads and invitations generated an attendance of about eight people. This was not the size of group that I wanted. To justify the costs of the seminar and my time for producing the program, I would need to gain a couple of large clients who would agree to use my services. Obviously, I had not enticed enough people to attend. Something had been wrong with my approach. Eventually, I concluded that perhaps the title of my seminar didn't gain much interest. My seminar appeared to be the same as many already being conducted in this locale. It was time to explore some other way of marketing my program.

Six months later I produced the same seminar at the same location. This time I had changed the presentation title. I changed the title to: How to Sell Your Property Without Generating Current Income Taxes. The room was full. Essentially, the seminar was the same, but I added a couple of new slides at the beginning to discuss tax-deferred property sales.

I discussed ways to sell a business through use of an Employer Stock Option Plan (ESOP). I showed how property could be transferred to a Charitable Remainder Trust (CRT) that would produce income without immediate taxation. Moreover, some of the CRT income could even be offset for a few years by carry over tax deductions resulting from the original donation to the CRT. I also explained how like-kind exchanges could be used for real estate and business stock. (Under a like-kind property exchange, the property can be exchanged for another type of similar property without experiencing current taxation).

After discussing these types of transactions that generate deferred tax results, I showed the impact of federal estate taxes and state inheritance taxes on the assets they owned. These were the same types of topics that had been addressed in the earlier seminar, but the difference was that this time, the room was full. Several people approach me after the presentation to schedule follow-up discussions. Some of them were high net worth clients and my team was able to help them significantly.

So, what is the point of this story? My point is that if you are not getting the attendance you want from your seminar, you might not be marketing it properly. Check the title of your presentation. Does the title make you want to attend? Does it sound like a seminar frequently being presented in the area? Would you have more success with a better title or description? Make sure you submit any program you develop to your company's compliance department, though. If you are not trying to mislead the attendees, and the information you are covering is accurate, you should have no trouble getting your program approved.

My next point addresses seminar costs. As I stated earlier, costs related to seminars can be high. You want to try to keep the costs low without decreasing the effectiveness of your program. Your goal is still to try to gain as many new clients as possible. And, you want the new clients to fit the profile of the type of client you are seeking. This is important. Why? Because you want your prospect to be someone that might have an interest in your product and you want a prospect that you are qualified to meet and serve. Let's look at an example. For illustration purposes I'll use a marketing medium you may have already used: direct mailing. Then, I'll tie that back to seminar selling.

Let's assume you are a 28-year-old sales rep with two years of experience. You have been trained to approach prospects that are around your age, and you lead with a life insurance product. There's nothing wrong with that. You will find prospects with this type of need. Now, let's further assume that you have not studied too many other financial services products and how they work.

You've noticed that one of your colleagues makes a lot more money than you by serving people in medical industries. You overlook the fact that she is 55 years old with 25 years of experience. You decide that this is a market that you want to be involved in, so you decide to undertake a direct mail campaign. You decide that your target market will be dentists. You purchase a mailing list and begin sending out materials.

Soon you discover that you are getting a good response to your mailing. You start to schedule appointments. The first dentist you meet is 62-years-old. He wants you to evaluate his retirement plan, but you have no experience with qualified plans. You will have to try to get someone with expertise in qualified retirement plans to accompany you to sales meetings with this client. What you don't see is that this prospect is thinking how can someone twenty-eight years old even relate to what I want? You might be brilliant at this topic but the dentist's perception is that he needs an older advisor. You have wasted time meeting with this prospect.

The second prospect you meet with wants to address estate planning issues, but you have never worked with an estate planning case. Again, you need help. If you have help available to you, both these can be viable prospects. If not, you might not be contacting prospects with high probabilities of becoming clients. On the other hand, if your mailing is sent to dentists that are your age with problems you can address with your knowledge base, your odds of making a new client are higher. You should always decide the profile of the prospect you want to approach. As you gain more knowledge in different financial services arenas, you will expand your prospect profiles because you will be qualified to serve their needs.

Determining a prospect profile is simply deciding what the prospect will look like. Are you seeking business owners? Are you trying to find married couples around your age? Do you want prospects with children? Is your best prospect someone thinking about retiring? You establish the parameters for the most efficient prospects related to your experiences. A couple of years from now you may need to revise your prospect profile because you will have gained more knowledge and can serve a broader base of people. Remember, when you invite people to one of your seminars, they should also be candidates that fit your prospect profile. After all, you are spending money to get them there, and you want the most bang for your buck.

Now, let's return to addressing seminar costs. I stated earlier that average seminar costs are around $5,000. Therefore, it is important to get the right people to attend. You don't want to have attendees that are simply looking for a free meal. It's like the mailings people get for a free trip to the Bahamas. Some people have no intention of buying a time share in the Bahamas. But, they are willing to sit through a presentation to get the free trip. You could find yourself in the same boat. You could have attendees who only wanted to see how good the food is at the restaurant you chose. You need to be selective. Maybe a slightly different and creative approach should be considered. Let me illustrate this point.

I once visited with a sales rep that came up with an innovative arrangement to get people to come to his seminar, and it didn't involve buying people a meal. He also did not need to rent a room for the presentation. The cost was the same as a normal seminar, but the attendance he got was huge.

This rep checked into the cost of having a major sports figure speak to a group of attendees. I don't remember who he used, but I believe it was a famous college football coach. I can relate to his thought process, because my wife is a huge Nebraska Cornhuskers fan. (Maybe I should not have said "huge." Perhaps "dedicated" would have been better.). At any rate, if she was told she could go hear Tom Osbourne for free, she would definitely try to attend. This sales rep applied this logic to his seminar. He figured if people could come and hear the famous coach for free, they would. He ended up being right.

He learned that the normal speaking fee of the coach in the local area was $5,000. Thus, the cost would be about the same as a regular seminar at a restaurant. Could he find a place to hold the meeting without too much room rent? He and his staff researched what was available in his area. There was a new public library in town and it had a large auditorium that held a little over 300 people. Because the new library wanted the public to become aware of this service that it could provide, he was offered the room at no cost. Now he had a seminar that would cost about the same as a regular seminar, but he could invite 300 prospects.

His seminar was a success. More than 300 people came. When the coach was finished speaking, the sales rep took about fifteen minutes to discuss who he was and the types of services his organization could offer. People were impressed that he knew the local hero coach. Their perception was that his firm must be really special to arrange a program like this. After all, this was the man who scheduled a meeting with one of their gods. A man that could get this person to speak at his seminar must be pretty skilled.

He had changed his seminar parameter a little, but it produced great results. See what a little creativity can get done? What can you do to make your seminar more efficient? I'm sure that with a little thought, you will come up with an answer. Again, make sure your company's compliance department is on board with any approach that you choose to employ.

Another factor that affects the attendance you will have at your seminar is prospect perception. I joined forces with another sales rep to present specific topics to CPAs (at one seminar) and to doctors (at the other seminar). For CPAs, we presented information on how to avoid the 10% penalties imposed on qualified plan distributions when taken before the plan participant reached age 59 ½. For doctors, we explained important aspects related to estate planning, an important topic for many of them because they often generate high net worth. The city we were in had more than 4,000 of these prospects. We sent out invitations to our free seminars. We got a small turnout (less than twenty out of four thousand).

We could not figure out what had gone wrong. Why was our turnout so low? We sought the opinion of a friend that often conducted seminars. He suggested that the reason our turnout was small was the perceptions of the people we invited. Our seminar was free. Most of us have attended free programs before and found they contained little value. Apparently our invitees had made this same assumption. They applied an old adage - You get what you pay for. Even though our presenters were highly credentialed, our invitees determined that something that was free probably did not offer much value.

We decided to see if a slightly different approach would produce better results. We waited six months and sent out invitations again. The same credentialed speakers were shown as the presenters. But this time we charged a fee of $125 for the program. We filled the room almost immediately. In fact, we had to turn people away. It seemed that, because we charged a fee for the program, invitees perceived that the seminar had value.

You can offer value in a number of ways to increase attendance. For Certified Financial Planners (CFPs), CPAs, Enrolled Agents, Lawyers, etc. you can offer continuing education credits. I have often produced seminars providing CE credits and had excellent attendance. The value to me was that many of the attendees gained knowledge of my skills and knew they could contact me to consult on cases or serve their clients.

Another valuable lesson I have learned from doing seminars is that a seminar has value if the topic covered has appeal. Some topics always have some appeal (retirement planning, estate planning, etc.). That's why so many people are doing them.

But, my greatest seminar successes have come from "hot" topics. Something brought the topic to the forefront and people wanted to know more about it. Perhaps people heard about the topic from a mailing, a television program, a newspaper article, a magazine article, or a friend.

One useful "hot" topic for me was the introduction of the Roth IRA (available after 1/1/97). Almost every media form mentioned these IRA accounts and people wanted to learn about them. I decided to offer a program describing how these products functioned. Shortly after Roth IRAs were introduced, I was traveling around the country teaching financial services reps about them. Locally, I was producing seminars to define their features and benefits.

Roth IRAs had appeal because they were designed to provide a tax-free retirement income. Furthermore, Roth income in retirement did not affect the taxation of social security benefits. That's right. When certain types of income reach specified limits, social security benefits become taxable. Roth IRA income has no impact on social security benefits. A Roth owner does not get an income tax deduction for contributions into the Roth, but, if certain conditions are met, income after age 59 ½ is tax-free. Income from all the growth is tax-free as well.

Now, I'm going to be honest with you. At the time when Roth IRAs first came out the limit that one could put into the account was $2,000 per year. One would have to sell an enormous amount of Roth IRAs to generate much income. I knew immediately that I could not sell enough of them in a year to provide my spouse the living standard she desired. But that did not bother me, because I've never really been a product provider. I take pride in providing my prospects and clients with financial plans. Everything the client owns needs to be integrated to assure his or her financial goals are met. My Roth IRA seminars were designed to help me gain clients, not product sales.

Each time I completed a seminar on Roth IRAs, people from the audience would approach me. Many would state that they wanted to purchase a Roth. I would explain, "I will be happy to help you acquire a Roth, but we really need to make sure that the product is right for you. There may be better alternatives for you, but to determine that we need to prepare a detailed financial plan. We need to make sure the Roth meshes well with your other financial products." I would point to my assistant at the back of the room and explain that they could schedule a financial planning appointment with her. I further explained that she would provide them a list of items we needed, and she would give them forms to complete before our first meeting.

When the attendee insisted he or she did not want an appointment for a financial plan, but only wanted to buy a Roth, I would explain that my assistant at the back of the room could help them pick out a product and complete the application. In those situations when we prepared a financial plan for one of these new clients, we discovered other financial gaps that needed to be addressed. Usually, we gained a long-term client that we could continue to serve. Some even produced nice referrals.

If you have been collecting clients using seminar selling, I'm sure that you have learned lessons I have not addressed here. I think seminars, when properly orchestrated, can produce very good results and help find quality clients. I am an advocate of their use. However, I always encourage sales reps to seek ways to make them more efficient and cost-effective. Properly structured, a seminar can lead to qualified clients who, in turn, will be excellent sources for referrals. If you are not using this sales technique, you should consider it.

OPENING A DIALOGUE

No progress is made in any human interaction without communication. A dialogue must be opened and continued. It doesn't matter whether the relationship is with a family member, a business associate, a business manager, a sales rep, or an individual seeking a soulmate. Interaction begins with a dialogue.

Is it difficult to start a dialogue? For most people it is not. It's probably not hard for you either, although this is one of the statements most sales reps regularly tell me. They ask if there is any easy way to get a dialogue going with a prospect.

Opening a dialogue is probably something you do many times a week. For example, you meet your friend Sue, and ask, "What's happening, Sue?" Or, maybe you ask, "How are you and your family?" If she responds to whatever question you ask, the dialogue has started. Information Sue imparts helps to continue the dialogue. Your next question or comment will be based on how she responded.

You start dialogues everyday with your work associates. You

202

might relate how terrible your last phone call was. You might comment on another employee's outfit not being fit for work. Perhaps you are exhorting the features of a new product. Or, again, you might be asking a fellow employee for his or her thoughts on a subject. If you are a manager, you might be asking for an update from an employee on a specific project. If you ask someone to show you how a computer program works, you have started a dialogue. In each of these scenarios an attempt to start a dialogue occurs.

A dialogue does not need to be oral. It can be in the form of letters. Today's common format is via emails or texts. I have sent letters, emails, and texts to friends to catch up on what they are doing and how they are feeling. My cell phone allows me to text them for a quick update. Or, I can call them, but most the time I just get their voicemail. However, I have had effective conversations by leaving them voicemails and by receiving voicemails back. I've had complete conversations without ever directly talking to friends or clients.

I am always surprised to hear people who seem to have no trouble visiting with acquaintances tell me that they have difficulty starting conversations. Yet, they do it all the time. I have to assume that they have some hang up about the process. I believe they are making the process more difficult than it actually is. These same people can be at a party and simply introduce themselves. "Hi, I'm Steve." Usually the other individual will reciprocate. "Hi, my name is Phil."

"Do you live around here, Phil?" Then, "Where do you work?" Also, "Do you have children?" You get the picture. It is not hard to have these types of conversations. You have them all the time.

For quick encounters with people, you need to have some prepared information to deliver, especially when people ask you where you work or what you do for a living. In the financial services industry we call this prepared information the "elevator speech." This is a short statement that informs someone what you do in a couple of sentences. It is what you might tell someone who asks you the question on an elevator. You have the amount of time it takes to get from the twelfth floor to the first floor to respond. You want to tell just enough information in the allotted amount of time to make them want more information. You want them to ask for more details. You want them to say, "How do you do that?" Then, you can try to set up a time to discuss it further. There are short articles online about how to develop an "elevator speech." Simply google the topic and take a few minutes to read about it. Then take a couple more minutes to create your own elevator speech.

Depending on the new acquaintance's answers to where he or she works and what products you offer, you can simply ask if their company uses those types of products. Be tactful in how this is done. You must let them know that you are not just trying to sell them something. They need to know you want to develop a relationship that is mutually beneficial to both of you.

If you sell cars, you might ask what kind of vehicle they are looking for. You might ask, "Joe, how's that car I sold you a few years ago holding up? Is it time to update your vehicle?" If you sell computers, it is helpful to find out how the device is used and how long they have had it. If you offer sporting goods, knowing which sports they are involved with directs you to product lines in which they have an interest. If you provide financial services, an indication of their goals and how they are trying to achieve them is helpful.

Years ago, I spent time working with a financial advisor for a couple of days. When he met someone he knew (he lived in a fairly small town and we would run into people at restaurants and stores) he would ask, "Bill, how are you doing? Are you still working at the same job?" Then he would ask something like, "How many days left until you retire?" It did not matter how old the person was. I saw him ask this question to a thirty-five year old. A couple of hours later, he asked a fifty-five year old. It usually got a response that opened up further dialogue.

On another occasion I saw an advisor walk into a restaurant, pull out a folder with sample insurance ledgers, select one that was close to the age of a restaurant customer, and lay it on the table beside the customer. (The ledger had many disclaimers on it indicating that it was only an illustration. It stated that an accurate ledger needed to be prepared for the customer). Then, the advisor and I sat down at another table and had lunch. I was surprised at how many times a customer finished his lunch and approached us with questions about the ledger. After answering a few questions, the advisor would suggest he and the customer get together. It was a simple approach, but it worked. If you sell cars, you might give the person a brochure showing your products.

When the individual responds to your question, it opens the door for you to ask clarifying questions. These types of questions help you zero in on what the client really wants. You might not have the time to answer a lot of questions at that moment, but you can ask if you can call to set up an appointment for further discussions.

Clarifying questions provide more data for you to use to help the client find a solution. If you sell cars and have just asked the individual if he or she is about ready to replace their old car, you can ask, "Are you looking for the same type of vehicle, or are you considering a model change? Has your family outgrown the model you're in? Are you trying to get a smaller model to lower fuel costs? Do you need something that will tow an RV or a boat?" The client's answers will clarify what he or she desires or needs. You need the additional information to provide the best solution for the customer.

If you sell retirement plans to businesses, you would want to know: if the business has a retirement plan already? If so, what type of plan does the business have? Is the existing plan performing to the owner's satisfaction? Do the employees like the plan? Is there something the business does not like about it?

I have discussed various types of questions for opening dialogues and gathering information in other chapters of this book, so I am not going to give a total review of them again. I will, however, mention a couple of types. I have discussed the "clarifying" question in this section. You simply ask for clarification. Did you mean… The "vision" questions ask the client to pretend he or she is in the future and describe what the business or family looks like. "Open-ended" questions make the client provide more details than a closed-ended question. Closed-ended questions can be answered with as little as one or two words. Open-ended questions cannot be answered with only a couple of words. See the chapter titled "The Perfect Question" for examples.

I guess the point I am trying to make is that many people think that opening a dialogue with someone is very difficult. But, they are overthinking the process. They open dialogues every day. If you believe starting a dialogue is difficult, you need to develop a question, or list of questions, to ask. The questions you use might vary depending on the age of the person you address. Young couples with children might need to be asked about education plans for the children. Middle-aged individuals could be approached about how long they have until retirement. Retired people might be interested in annuities or Medicare supplement policies and a question related to those topics would suffice. Whatever your product line, you can create a one-line question to start a dialogue. If you are having difficulty creating an opening question, talk to the mentors in your organization. Their experiences have helped them develop techniques for opening dialogues. They can share advice regarding the questions they use and why they use them. Take advantage of the sources available to you. What works for them may work for you too.

THE CLIENT'S OTHER ADVISORS

I had not been in the financial services industry for very long before I learned the importance of working with the client's other financial advisors. If the client has a strong relationship with an attorney or CPA, the client will do what they tell him or her to do, even if it isn't in their best interest. These professionals are not trying to lead the client astray – sometimes they do not have experience in the field you and the client are discussing. For example, if the attorney regularly works with divorces, property documents, income tax settlements, etc., he or she may not be versed in estate tax laws. Or, if the CPA spends times auditing the client's accounting records, he or she may be unaware of specific tax rules (e.g., tax advantages from retirement plans). Nonetheless, the client may place a premium value on the guidance of these advisors.

In one of my early cases, I worked with a client to structure a life insurance program to provide funds to cover his estate taxes. Without the insurance these taxes would greatly diminish the estate when he died. His assets were not liquid and would undoubtedly need to be sold at reduced values to cover the tax. He told his accountant about the life insurance. His accountant said that he did not need the insurance because the client's heirs could use section 6166 of the internal revenue code. This IRS provision allows for the estate tax to be paid over several years in installment payments.

The accountant had not taken into account the fact that the business operation did not have significant cash flow. In lean years the living owner had to engage in creative management to get by. The owner's heirs did not have the business knowledge the current owner possessed. Lean years after the father was gone would probably put them out of business. This happens to inherited businesses all the time. The heirs would still owe the estate tax, so the business property would probably still need to be sold to pay the tax debt. Then, the heirs would no longer have the business to produce their livelihoods. The accountant was a good bookkeeper, but did not understand the family dynamics. Most accountants are not very good with scenarios involving psychology.

Initially, I blamed the accountant for the loss of this sale. In reality, the fault was mine. I should have involved the accountant in discussions from the onset. I could have made him look like an expert whose advice was invaluable. Had I said something like, "Mr. Accountant, I know you are aware that the federal tax laws provide ways to pay estate taxes through installments, but I also know that you are aware of the weaknesses in these arrangements. After the business owner dies, the heirs usually do not have as much knowledge about the business as he did. That's why statistics show that most inherited businesses fail. The use of life insurance to cover the estate taxes takes some pressure off of the heirs and increases the business's chance of survival.

"Additionally, a strong cash value policy can provide an asset for the business, and this makes banks happy when the client needs a loan. But, I'm not telling you anything you don't already know. Your role is important in this plan because you will help the client pay the premiums and you will reflect the policy values on the business books." By not involving the accountant in my discussions with the client, he viewed me as a threat and was unwilling to endorse my proposal.

There are times when I need to try to direct a client to a professional that is familiar with the solutions I am recommending. In these cases, I need to be careful that I don't affect the relationship the client has with their existing advisor. If the advisor thinks I am trying to do that, he or she will become an obstacle which I may not be able to overcome.

If I am working on an estate planning case involving wills, trusts, guardianships, etc., and I know the client's attorney does not regularly work in this arena, I will suggest the use of a specialist. Attorney shops with only one or two attorneys probably do not have this type of skilled lawyer. It will cost the client several hundred dollars to educate the attorney in a small shop. He will pay for many hours of research time, or he will get documents that are boilerplate documents that contain provisions not applicable to the client's situation. An attorney that already has the necessary experience will cost less because he or she will not need to charge for researching the regulations.

If the client uses a large law firm, a different law partner will usually be able to provide the knowledge needed. In large law firms, the attorneys usually specialize in specific arenas. One might work with property transactions. Another might specialize in collections. There might be one or two divorce attorneys. And, there might be an attorney that only works with estate planning situations.

I've found this to be true in my personal situations. I used small firms to collect unpaid rent on my rental properties. Usually, they did not have much luck in collecting rent that was in arrears. It took them three months to get the renter evicted, and I still did not get any rent. When I hired a large law firm, it had a specialist that only worked with collections. I got my rental unit back much more quickly, and the attorney garnished wages of those renters who had not paid. He was relentless. One woman who had lived in the state for thirty-four years had to leave the state so she would be in a jurisdiction in which he did not practice. Hiring the larger firm was much more profitable for me. When I needed an estate planning attorney, the same firm had a specialist in that field.

Some clients are reluctant to use only one financial advisor. It seems that the more wealth they have, the more advisors they want. I think this happens because the client is being cautious. They have been told often that they should not have all their eggs in one basket. Their grandfathers gave them this advice. So, when working with your clients, don't get too concerned if they have other advisors. If you do a good job for your client, you may get to handle some of the client's other investments. If you do a better job than the other advisor, you might get to handle more of the investments. However, your client needs to know that if you are preparing a financial plan, you need to know about all of the investments the client owns. Otherwise, your analysis will not be accurate.

When I have meetings with a client, I ask if there are other advisors we should involve in our planning. "Mr./Ms. Prospect, do you have an attorney or accountant that should be involved in our discussions? I know there will be a fee for their services but we should coordinate our decisions with the rest of your financial activities. After all, these professionals will need to prepare documents related to our solutions. If you do not have an attorney already, I can help suggest one or two for you to contact. By involving these individuals, we also make sure that anything we decide to do is in line with actions they have already taken."

If the client involves his or her CPA or attorney, I thank the professional for his or her involvement. I let the advisors know that I think their input is valuable. I assure them that I want to be certain that whatever we implement will be in line with the client's other activities. If they do not have the expertise needed for procedures we are discussing, I provide materials to help them learn. Or, I ask them if they would like to bring in another resource with whom they may have a relationship.

It is always better to involve the client's other advisors from the outset. In some instances, where an advisor has expertise beyond your skills, they will be able to teach you and direct your activities. They will be able to assure that beneficiary designations are correct, especially where there are trusts involved. Sometimes wills create trusts at the moment of death to hold assets for minor children. An expert attorney can oversee the documents you complete.

Bringing the client's advisors to the table also makes them an associate instead of an adversary. Let them know that you value their expertise. Make sure they know that they are the instruments in the client's orchestra, and you are only the conductor. Your goal is that everyone involved be in harmony.

DIVERGENCE

I have a friend that has a relative who seeks to control all family situations. If several family members get together for a celebration and they agree to go out to dinner, this relative indicates opposition to the restaurant everyone has agreed to patronize. It's not because she does not like the restaurant chosen - it's about control. On any other day she might patronize the restaurant, but this time she resists. She wants to make sure everyone knows she has power. In reality, her behavior simply upsets everyone in the family. She is invited to fewer family gatherings every year, and the family members do not visit her as frequently as they visit other family members. The prevailing opinion is that she is simply "not worth the trouble."

Another friend of mine has a relative whose wallet seems to be welded in his pocket. This relative never offers to pay for anything. He knows that if he doesn't offer to pay, someone else will. He will order something from the menu that he has never had before (usually one of the most expensive items) and then complain about it as he eats it. He also is adamant about not wanting to go to an Italian restaurant, but if you take him to a restaurant that has one Italian dish on the menu, that is the item he will order. After someone at the table has paid the check he will often say, "You did not need to pay the check. I was going to do that." The next time he is taken to dinner, he uses the same tactic. Because of this trait most family members just feed him a meal at their home. Paying for a meal that he complains about is simply no longer worth it to his family.

Years ago I had a neighbor that was pretty successful. He had no reservations about telling his neighbors about his success. His neighbors referred to him as boastful. One of the neighbors who had recently been laid off was going through some trying times of unemployment. He avoided this neighbor any chance he got. Listening to the neighbor brag about his success did not help the unemployed person's self-esteem. He said the successful neighbor's boasting made him feel bad. Eventually, the unemployed neighbor determined that listening to the boastful neighbor simply wasn't worth the trouble.

I once worked with a co-worker that was a hypochondriac. The last thing you wanted to ask her was, "How are you?" She would tell you. She would recite all the conditions she had and then add a few more that she thought she had. After asking her how she was a couple of times, people learned not to ask her again. They simply said, "Hi," and walked on. Some even said that having a conversation with her was "not worth the trouble."

I am sure that most of you can relate to these stories. Every family seems to have some member like these. We tolerate many things with family members that we would never tolerate from someone else. If a "friend" treated us like this, the friendship would suffer. We would eventually cease to spend much time with that individual.

If one of our employees did not grant us respect, we would probably phase out their position. Or, we would make the job challenging enough that he or she might give notice and go elsewhere. I have seen bosses use these strategies.

Sometimes it is necessary for individuals to diverge. That is, they must branch off in different directions. They simply are not a match. And, remaining in the relationship is not healthy for either of them. They do not need to get angry about the issues, simply spend less time together. Perhaps the relationship needs to be severed for the benefit of both of them.

So why am I discussing this subject? It is because similar situations can exist with clients. It takes so much work to acquire most clients that we often tolerate some client behaviors that we shouldn't. We think we must maintain the relationship because they produce part of the revenue stream on which we live. In reality, the amount of time we spend on some of these clients greatly impacts the profitability of our business. Some clients require so much of our time that it affects our ability to acquire new clients. Spending a large amount of time on key clients may be acceptable. But, I have had clients with very small investments who call me almost every day. I realize they are worried about their money, but some simply waste time. Some call simply because they are lonely.

As businessmen and businesswomen, it is necessary for us to

evaluate each client and determine what category he or she is in. Does he or she produce adequate profit for the time devoted to them? Would the client be better served working with another advisor? Could the client's concern be that they really do not respect or trust you and the services you provide? I never want to abandon a client, but sometimes it is necessary to help a client find another advisor with whom they feel more comfortable. Let me give you an example.

As a financial advisor, I am asked questions about all types of investments, even those I do not offer. I always let my client know I do not offer that type of investment, but since I am an Enrolled Agent (designation granted by the IRS), I can answer tax questions about the investment. I have one particular client in the medical profession that asks me tax questions, and when I give him the correct answer, he argues with me about the information I have provided. I end up having to provide him copies from the tax code to prove my answer is correct. I find this very frustrating. If it happened occasionally with this client I could understand it. But, it happens all the time. Obviously, he does not respect my credentials and knowledge. He takes too much of my time for the profit he generates. Eventually, I had a discussion about our relationship.

"Doctor," I said, "You are a very talented professional. I value your diagnoses. So do many other patients of yours. That's why your patients ask you questions about their health and follow your advice. I'm sure you rarely have a patient argue with you about your diagnosis or question your skill. On the other hand, every time you ask me a question, you disagree with my answer. It appears that you do not trust my judgement. I definitely want you to feel comfortable with your financial advisor. I want you to sleep soundly at night. Therefore, I am recommending a couple of other financial advisors you should consider." I gave him a couple of names to contact. I do not know who he ended up with, but the advisor's names I provided are very good. I no longer have to spend time researching and copying tax code to show that I am a competent advisor.

I call this "firing a client." It is one of the hardest things I had to learn to do. In this competitive profession it takes time to add a quality client. That is why it is so hard to terminate a client relationship. I take this process very seriously. However, I have discovered that some clients simply "aren't worth the trouble."

I know there are circumstances that can affect your ability to terminate a client relationship. If the client is your father-in-law, you may need to simply bite the bullet. This is one of the reasons I usually do not have business relationships with relatives. I want them to be properly served so I help them find a good advisor. I do not want a business relationship to affect our personal relationship.

If you practice in a very small community, terminating a client relationship can impact your reputation. The client will tell his or her side of the story to his neighbors. He or she may not be too complimentary of your action. If you are able to charge a fee for financial advice, this may help reduce the number of times the client calls. You may have to employ this technique to limit the client's contacts. Otherwise, you may simply have to sit down with the client and discuss what you can and cannot do for him or her. In larger cities, it will be easier for you to help your client find another competent advisor.

Only you can determine the value of each client, but it is important for you to evaluate your client base. Some clients will provide a good income stream. Some will provide great referred leads. Some will stay with you even if their investments have a bad year, because they know that you have been good for them in the past. But some of them will take too much time – they will simply not be worth the trouble of having them as a client. As hard as it will be, you need to consider a divergent path from them. Long term, it will be better for both of you.

Another relationship you must evaluate is the one you have with your company. Over my career I have seen companies experience financial difficulties. Some have even declared bankruptcy. If you only sold for one of these companies you probably had a lean year or two when they went under. You may have been forced to seek out a relationship with another company. Perhaps you chose to represent more than one company after the bankruptcy.

When I started in the insurance business, I was with a small company. It had great ratings and was financially solid. The company offered great support to its sales reps and had an excellent reputation. It also provided excellent training for its producers. But, because it was fairly small, its product line was limited. I enjoyed the company and its personnel, but found that I was often challenged to provide the right product to fit my client's needs. I ended up forcing one of the company products into the solution. My solution for the client was the proverbial square peg in a round hole.

Eventually, prospects and clients began asking for products my company did not offer (e.g., mutual funds, variable annuities, long term care, etc.). I knew it was time to seek out other company relationships or I would begin losing clients. Once a client seeks out another producer for assistance, the products you have sold them are at risk of replacement. Since the company I was associated with was a captive agency organization (it did not allow me to sell other company's products), I had to sever my relationship with it. I hated to do it, but I had to in order to survive.

The company I had been with was eventually absorbed by another. My original company did not have the capital to expand its product line. The acquisition of my company by another improved the product mix of both companies. Had I owned a crystal ball showing my company's future, I might have stayed with my company. In the long run, my divergence to other companies was a good move. I gained access to more products, more training, more sales materials, name-brand recognition, and expert support in advanced marketing.

Today, it is not as difficult for financial advisors to offer a broader product mix. Most companies recognize that a sales rep has to serve his or her client's needs. Companies recognize that if the sales rep does not have an adequate product mix to serve the client's needs, the client may seek out another advisor that does. To help their sales reps offer more product lines, many companies form relationships with other companies that offer products they cannot afford to create. In other words, if the sales rep's company does not offer a product line the rep needs, the company signs an agreement with another company to permit its sales reps to sell the other company's products.

In some instances, companies do not object to their sales rep selling products offered by other companies, especially if the product line is one they do not provide. Many companies even allow a sales rep to sell other company products they offer, too. An example can be seen in annuity markets. It is not uncommon for annuity sales reps to represent several different companies. Interest rates or product features change constantly on annuity products and representing several companies allows the sales rep the ability to better serve a client's needs.

If you are a specialist that only sells one product line, such as Medicare supplement products, you probably have an adequate relationship with your company and do not need to consider a change. I have a friend who only sells Disability Insurance. She has one of the best DI products available for her clients. For probably thirty years she has made a good living selling disability policies and nothing else. Maybe your situation is similar. Only you can determine if your company affiliation is adequate. If it is, go ye therefore and prosper. If your company affiliation is not serving your clients' needs, it might be time for divergence. Or, it might at least be time to add the products you need to your current product mix.

One producer I know became the top producer with his company.

This was a problem for his manager, the one who had hired him. Before this sales rep became the top producer for the company, his manager had been the top producer. Instead of simply enjoying the success of his protégé, the manager displayed symptoms of jealousy. The recognition the manager had received for being the top producer was now being lavished on someone else. This manager could have simply enjoyed the override commissions he received from the sales rep's activity, which were more than his own commissions, but the green-eyed monster kept his joy confined.

It did not take anyone long to recognize that the relationship between these two was strained. Visitors to the office picked up on the uncomfortable vibes that were prevalent. Something needed to be done. It was similar to a marriage beginning to go bad. You could not put your finger on what was happening, but you sensed that things were not amicable. A divorce was on the horizon, and needed to happen for the health of the manager and his sales representative.

Eventually, the sales rep left to represent another company. Because he was a top producer, he had many offers. After the sales rep left, his manager returned to being the top producer in his company, and the sales rep went to a new company and became its top producer. These individuals are no longer good friends but each is happier in his current environment. If you and your manager cannot work out your difficulties, both of you are probably not as happy as you could be. It may be time for divergence.

Severing any relationship is difficult, but sometimes it is necessary for both parties involved. If you are unhappy, you will probably make uncomplimentary statements about the other party. Terminating the relationship may be best for both of you. Most of us know a married couple who were verbally or physically abusive to each other. While it was difficult for us to watch them go through the divorce process, it ended up being good for both of them to separate. I remember attending churches where congregation members said we should pray for the divorcing couple to get back together. My life experiences have taught me otherwise. I now pray that the couple be lead to do whatever is best for the both of them.

If you are thinking about ending a relationship, you should probably seek advice and counsel from others. Outside counsel does not need to be an attorney. It can be other business associates or friends. External advice can often provide insight to help you make the right choice. Sometimes outside counsel can help you discover what the problem really is, and if there is some other positive solution. Other times, it is simply necessary for divergence to occur. Consider all of your options before making a change. If change is needed, make the change quickly. It is like pulling off a band aid. The quicker it is done, the less the pain will be. Making the change might definitely be "worth the trouble."

IF YOU HIDE BEHIND SOMETHING...

I marvel at how we human beings are able to devise explanations for the bad things that happen to us. Our most common explanation is that someone or something else is to blame. If you don't believe that, you should have seen me at the bowling alley in my youth. When I was having a bad night, often it was because the lanes had been freshly waxed. Or, maybe the lanes needed waxing. It might have been that the temperature in the alley was so high that my fingers were sweating, and I could not get a good grip on the ball. Sometimes the humidity was so low that my fingers would not slide easily out of the bowling ball holes. Of course, it could have been the group in the adjoining lane whose rowdiness was affecting my concentration. You get the picture. It was hardly ever my fault, but someone else's.

I tried golf several years ago and discovered that everyone I played with was better. That made golf a very expensive sport for me. Usually, the parties in the foursome made wagers on their shots or putts. I think they asked me to join them because I helped fund their retirement plans. On bad days, the wind was often at fault. Sometimes the putting greens were too fast because they were too dry. Sometimes the greens were too slow due to dew. Maybe the grounds keeper had not properly mowed the course. Or, the new golf balls I was using didn't have enough bounce. Again, you can see it really wasn't my fault that I was a mediocre golfer.

The reality is that I knew in my subconscious where the problems were. I just did not want to acknowledge them. Today, I'm a little better at accepting responsibility for my own ineptitude. It's still hard to say "I was wrong" or "I'm sorry," but those words will pass my lips more often as I age. I can also admit that someone is better than me. There are better sales reps, better tax nerds, better number crunchers, and I am okay with that.

For me, it is fascinating to hear explanations others come up with to describe why things are not working out for them. Undoubtedly, you hear them in conversations with your prospects, clients, friends, and family. If you are like me, you often have to "bite your tongue" and keep your comments to yourself, even though that can be very challenging.

A friend of mine in the financial services industry always tells me she wants a better job. She has a good job right now but is clearly overworked. She doesn't mind hard work but her job doesn't give her any free time. She even has to complete projects on weekends. I tend to agree that she needs a different job. When I ask her how many resumes she has sent out she says, "Two."

When I was laid off from a job at age forty I sent out three hundred resumes in about ten days. I heard many of the same rejections others hear: You are overqualified. We need someone to locate to another city. Your salary demands will be high enough that you'll take another job as soon as one is available, etc. However, I received seven job offers in six weeks. I was not interested in some of them, but at least I had those options. Eventually, I accepted one of the offers and started employment a couple weeks later. Maybe my friend would have more success finding another job if she sent out more resumes.

I have a relative who always complains about finding a job, too. He applies for jobs that require more education that he has. Moreover, he doesn't seem to want to devote the time needed to get the appropriate knowledge. These days the employment market is very competitive. Some of the jobs I applied for when I was looking had three hundred applicants. If you come in second, you still don't get the job. It's hard to compete for a position when other applicants have more skills or education.

I have heard sales reps state that the reason they have trouble meeting production numbers is that the products they are given to sell are not competitive. Yet, the top producer with their company makes two million dollars per year selling the same products. Maybe it would be wise to find out how other successful reps are selling those products. Maybe those same techniques can be used by you if your production is not where you want it to be.

Along these same lines, sometimes employees say they were inadequately trained to be doing a good job. Yet, all of the other employees (or sales reps) who were in the same class are doing well. Maybe the supervisor can arrange for individual training to provide the needed skills. It wouldn't hurt to ask.

Another reason I often hear from employees is that my boss doesn't like me. That's why I never get promoted. That's why I never get a good raise. It's because I am experiencing discrimination. I know it is because of my tattoo. But, across the aisle is an attorney with a big tattoo who is highly regarded. It's because I am a woman. But, one of the Vice Presidents is a woman. I think it's because of my religion. But, the boss has never discussed religion. I'm not going to say that these forms of discrimination do not exist. They do. And, maybe it is true for you. However, in most cases what I have learned is that when a person brings value to a business, none of these other factors are important. Maybe this employee needs to concentrate on how to increase his or her value.

The reason my sales suffer compared to the other sales reps is that the company gave me the worst territory. It's interesting because our top sales rep had that territory before you and did extremely well. Perhaps it's time to find out how he or she served the clients in that territory. That information might make you more effective.

The boss gives all the cushy jobs to the other employees. Why? Is it because they have more knowledge and experience? Is it because the customers always give them good reviews and ask for them? Employers love employees that have great attitudes and work hard. Maybe the employee needs to do a self-analysis to determine if he or she is the type of employee they would hire if they owned the company.

The commissions the company pays me are just too low to make a living. If that is true, you might be with the wrong company. It may be time to consider employment elsewhere. After all, you are in control of your life. Companies are always looking for good sales representatives. If you are a good sales rep, you will not have any trouble getting a job elsewhere. You owe it to yourself to get all you can from your job, if you are giving all you can.

An ostrich buries its head in the sand when it does not want to see a danger. He is still visible to others in the world but in his mind, he is hidden. I am reminded of my little Scottie dog (See the chapter titled Ali vs Tyson) when I think about this.

When I scold Beam me (my Scotty's name – short for Beam Me Up), he runs through the pet door to the rear of the backyard and hides behind an ash tree. Even though the young ash tree is only four inches in diameter he feels he is adequately hidden. He is twenty inches long, not counting the tail, so eight inches sticks out on one side of the tree and eight inches is revealed on the other. He seems to feel safe, like he cannot be seen. He is using the tree to hide behind but it is simply not big enough to cover him. That's how I feel about most excuses.

Most people can see right through excuses. They may not say anything, but they are thinking it, like in the examples I have given above. If they know you, they probably know the reason why you use the excuse.

Those of you who know me know that I am an amputee from an

accident that occurred to me in my childhood. It would be so easy for me to despair about my loss of fingers and use it to explain why the world is so unfair to me. Had I done that, I would not have ridden a motorcycle more than one hundred thousand miles in my life. I would have not learned to play guitar and enjoyed jamming with some musicians from Jimmy Buffet's band, Ray Charles band, or Kansas when I lived in Topeka. I never played with these bands – I had my own – but I got to pick and grin with some of their musicians.

Furthermore, I would never have undertaken writing this book. After all, everyone knows that a person missing fingers from a hand cannot type. But, this is my second book. It takes me longer than most able typists, but I was committed to writing my books. If you are committed to something, you will accomplish it as well. It is up to you to determine what you want your commitment to be. Once you determine what that is, work hard to achieve it.

If you decide you do not know what you want to do and can't make a commitment, you'll always have explanations or excuses to cover you. Just remember, if you are going to hide behind an excuse, make sure it's big enough to cover you.

BABY GATES

I'm sure you have probably been to seminars to hear a motivational speaker. If so, you have probably heard stories about how a mind can be conditioned to set limitations on itself. One example often used is about baby elephants. The baby elephant is chained to a stake when it is young. It pulls and tugs on the stake it is attached to, but it is not big enough to pull the stake free. It eventually gives up and accepts that is has a limited range in which it can travel. Later, when it is a full-grown elephant it can be attached to the same stake – which it could easily pull out of the ground – and it will not try to pull away from the stake. It has been conditioned to believe that it cannot pull the stake free, so it doesn't even try. The fully-grown elephant continues to be limited to a world that extends to the end of the chain.

Perhaps you have also heard about the experiment that scientists conducted using two fish: a barracuda and a mackerel. Both were placed in the same fish tank. Normally, a barracuda will attack a mackerel and eat it. In this experiment, a glass partition was used to divide the fish tank in half. The barracuda kept trying to attack the mackerel but continuously bumped into the invisible barrier created by the glass. Eventually, the barracuda gave up. Even after the scientists removed the glass partition from the tank the barracuda and mackerel occupied the same tank without incident. The barracuda had been conditioned to know it could not swim to the other side of the tank.

For my illustration of how limitations develop in minds, I need to remind you that two dogs occupy my house with my wife, a cat, and me. For more details about them, see the story titled "Ali vs. Tyson." Our animals (and my wife) are pretty spoiled. All of them are usually able to convince me to give them what they want.

Before we got a pet door that fits in our patio door, we had to open the patio door to let our pets out whenever they wanted to go outside. Once the patio door was opened, our pets could go outdoors and play or use the backyard as their litter box. Once they discovered we would stop what we were doing and slide the door open, they were relentless. They abused their power. It seemed like they wanted to go out every few minutes.

Since we were not sure what their reasons for wanting to go outside were – they might have needed to use the outdoor litter box - we obeyed their commands. Unfortunately, most the time they just wanted to go outside and bark at a squirrel or neighbor walking by with his or her dog. It did not take long for this process of opening the patio door whenever they commanded us to become annoying. We were opening the patio door several times a day. We realized that we needed another option. We needed to get a pet door. That would allow our animals to go in and out without our assistance. We could continue relaxing when they wanted to go out. We searched the internet and found a suitable pet door. We ordered it immediately.

We were not sure the pets would use the door. We had been told that after living a few months pets have developed enough fears that they are hesitant to try new things. They do not want to be exposed to danger. This is why pet experts often say that "you cannot teach an old dog new tricks." For the most part, this is true. If the dog has never used a pet door, it is unlikely that it will try to use one. We were desperate. We decided we needed to give the pet door a try. We thought our dogs would be curious enough to at least investigate the new device. Fortunately, we were right.

It took a little while, maybe 30 minutes, before our animals discovered they could go out through the pet door. Once one dog figured out how to use the pet door, the other dog followed. They entered and existed so many times the first couple of days that we thought they would wear out the door in a week. Eventually the novelty wore off and they learned to use it less frequently. For the most part they only use it as needed. Of course, they are the ones that determine when they think they need to use the door.

After watching the dogs go in and out regularly, the cat's curiosity was also stimulated. He gave it a try. He reached out and touched it with his paw and noticed it moved. He reached out again and experienced the same result. After a few minutes he was pushing his head against it, and it opened to reveal the outdoors. Being cautious, he would back into the house and wait a couple of minutes before trying the door again. It took about a half hour for him to go through. Then, at the first frightening sound he rushed back into the house. He continued this procedure for a couple of hours before feeling he could safely enter the back yard. After all, he had two brothers (the dogs) to protect him.

Now, they are all pet door experts. In many respects the pet door was a Godsend for us. When an animal needed to go out it could handle the situation itself. We could continue watching a TV show or finish another project while the animals went in and out on their own. The manufacturers of the pet door thought of the things a pet owner needed. If the animals need to be confined to the house (e.g., when the lawn care people come) there is a small metal door that can be inserted into grooves to restrict access to the outside. In other words they can be locked indoors.

Also, the pet door has magnets at its bottom. These help to keep it closed on a windy day. The magnets do not create a lot of resistance, so the pets can easily go through it. When one of our pets goes through the door the magnets click. When we hear it click, we know that one of the animals has just used the door.

The pet door creates a few minor problems for us, though. Since our pets can use the door whenever they want (unless the metal door is slid into the grooves), they can go out whenever they want to. So, if a neighbor walks by with another dog and our dogs see them through the patio door glass, they have a tendency to run outside and bark at the perceived intruder. They feel strongly about this because they feel we need to be protected. I guess I should be more accurate when describing this behavior. If anything walks by (e.g., a bunny rabbit, a ground squirrel, a bird, a shadow of a bird, etc.), our dogs perceive it as a threat to our safety. In those instances, they will run out and bark profusely. In those instances it sounds like we own a pack of wolves baying at the moon, yet it might be noon. Our next-door neighbor has repeatedly expressed his displeasure at this occurrence. To quell the noise we have to rise from the comfort of our armchairs, or discontinue whatever we are doing, and call them in, scold them, or insert the metal door until the temptation has passed.

But, the biggest problem caused by the pet door occurs when it rains. There are a couple of spots in the back yard where the grass does not grow – probably because our dogs are always policing the perimeter of our backyard, or are digging for treasure in those areas. After a soaking rain, those spots become muddy. Since our dogs believe they must guard the perimeter at all times, they stride right through the mud. Then, when they feel they have adequately protected our house, they return through the pet door. In those instances, they paint a mural on the kitchen floor with their muddy paws. If they go in and out several times to protect us, they paint a pretty large mud mural on the floor (or furniture). To prevent this from happening, we have installed baby gates in our kitchen to confine them to the area with a vinyl floor.

In case you don't know what a baby gate is, I should offer a definition. Baby gates are devices typically used to confine a baby in a room for its safety. They are often placed at the top of a stairway to prevent a baby from falling down the stairs. Or, they are placed in doorways to rooms containing something that might present a danger to the infant.

The baby gate we purchased fits in a doorway and can actually be latched shut. The latches are on top of the gates and make them more secure. The gates can only be opened if the latches are released. When we go through a gate, we pull it shut and latch it. At least we did when we first bought them. Since the baby gates are designed to create a barrier to keep children contained, they are sufficient to keep our dogs contained, as well. In fact, they work even better for our dogs. Without an opposable thumb they cannot open the latch. An older child might figure out how to open the latch.

Of course, when we first got the baby gates, our dogs had to test the limits of their new barriers. They tried to see how many times they could take a run at a gate and hit it before it opened. They tried hundreds of times, but fortunately, the latches held. Eventually, our dogs learned that the gate latches would not surrender. The cat is not as restricted by the gates because he can jump on top of them, and then jump down to the other side. We were not as concerned about the cat because he doesn't go out to bark at passersby, nor does he like to walk in mud.

Today, our dogs know they are restricted by the baby gates. We can pull the gates shut without latching them, and our dogs accept the fact that they are imprisoned. They have been conditioned to realize that the baby gates limit their access to the rest of the world. We can confine our dogs to the kitchen and backyard whenever we want. In their minds, they cannot escape the confines we have created. When the backyard is dry, we simply open the gates and give them the run of the house. But, while the gates are closed, the dogs know they cannot proceed beyond them, even if not latched. In a way, they have developed "baby gates" in their minds that tell them they cannot break through the barrier.

Now, I am going to digress and tell you about a pertinent personality trait that Beamie (short for Beam Me Up), the Scottish Terrier has. When he doesn't get his way, Beamie throws a hissy fit. He is an expert at throwing these fits. If there were an Olympic event for hissy fitting, he would be a contender for the gold medal. I'm sure that you have seen children throw great hissy fits. I've seen children lie on a department store floor, screaming and kicking their feet if they don't get the toy they asked for. You have seen incidents like this, too. Beamie has a similar personality. Beamie's form of tantrum is to grab a stuffed toy and shake it as hard as he can while growling like he is trying to kill it.

No one has ever seen a dog's head shake as fast as Beamie's when he's throwing a fit. In fact, one time he was so angry at a neighbor that walked her dog past our yard, that he broke a blood vessel in his right ear. He REALLY shook his stuffed animal. Soon after, the ear began to swell. When the ear reached the size of a small apple we took him to see the veterinarian. The vet told us Beamie would need surgery and scheduled it for the next day. The Vet said he needed to fuse some blood vessels together to stop the internal bleeding.

After the surgery, we picked up Beamie and took him home. Of course, he had to wear a "cone of shame" around his neck to keep him from scratching his ear. He hated the cone. He did not think it stylish enough for him. He kept trying to remove it. Fortunately, we were able to find a protective device that was like a life saver or inner tube. It was inflatable and went around his neck. Most pet stores have these in various sizes. It protected his ear from being scratched, but also provided a pillow for him to lie on. It was a nice, soft cushion. The vet told us that Beamie would need almost a month to heal. But, the vet did not know our dog's personality.

About three weeks after the surgery, Beamie was sitting in the back yard when another neighbor walked by with her two Retrievers. Again, Beamie felt the need to be protective. He grabbed a stuffed toy and threw the grand mal of hissy fits. He shook his head so vigorously, he re-injured his ear. The blood vessel was broken again, and his ear filled with blood again. The doctor had to do emergency surgery again. The second time, the vet reinforced the vessels enough to fix the problem. Even though hissy fits are still an important part of Beamie's life, he has not had another incident with his ear. However, the second surgery had a side effect. Beamie's right ear no longer stands up. He left ear does, but his right ear doesn't. He's still pretty cute, though.

Because the veterinarian's practice is fairly large, he has several rooms in which dogs are seen. There are several vets in his practice, so having several rooms allows them to treat several pets at the same time. For both of Beamie's surgeries, the doctor used the same operating room.

What's interesting today (a couple of years after the surgeries) is how Beamie's surgeries affected him. We can take Beamie to the vet's office, put him down on the floor and let him roam. He will enter and investigate any of the vet's rooms except the one in which both his surgeries were performed. You could say that Beamie has formed a "Baby Gate" about this particular operating room. He fears that if he goes into it, he will be uncomfortable and experience more pain. He remembers the discomfort and pain after his last two visits to that room. He probably doesn't want to wear the rubber "cone of shame" again. To prevent that from happening, Beamie simply avoids that room.

Human beings are not that different from my pets. We all have mental "baby gates" that limit us. Something in our past affects our behavior today. Maybe we:

- have had several bad relationships, so we've given up on relationships.

- as a child we were picked on by other kids, so we learned to avoid people.

- had a bad teacher who kept telling us we were stupid, and we've come to believe it.

- had a parent keep telling us we would never amount to anything, so we haven't.

- sit down to write something and hear a subconscious voice say it's not good enough.

You get the picture. Somewhere in our subconscious is a monster that tells us that if something makes us uncomfortable we should avoid it.

Even today, we all have our own mental baby gates, and they also affect us in business. We tried something a few times, maybe a certain form of prospecting, and didn't have success. We kept feeling more uncomfortable; so, we gradually started avoiding it. Now we avoid it completely.

We took an idea to our boss and he/she ridiculed it, so we don't take ideas to him or her anymore. Maybe if we kept trying a technique or presenting ideas (without being obnoxious about it, of course), success would come, but we'll never know because we no longer try.

I'm reminded of a story that Bill Harris, world famous annuity trainer, told at one of his seminars. [You can search for him on the internet and find out about his books and upcoming speaking engagements]. Bill said he was training his sales representatives to always ask a client if he/she had a pension or profit-sharing account, or an IRA somewhere. If you remember the old Columbo detective series from television, after an interview to gather evidence Columbo would always say, "Oh, just one more thing sir…" and ask the next question. Bill's approach was a lot like that. "Mr./Ms. Client, just one more thing, do you have a pension account or IRA that should be reviewed…".

One of his sales representatives told him he had tried this 5 times already, and the question produced no results. The sales representative said he wasn't going to ask the question again. He said it wasn't productive. This sales rep had formed a "baby gate" in his mind. He didn't feel comfortable asking people about their retirement assets, so that he wasn't going to ask anymore. Bill encouraged him to just keep trying it a few more times. Reluctantly, the sales rep agreed he would.

After the sales rep asked the question following his 8th client meeting, the client responded, "I'm glad you asked that. I've got a profit-sharing account with over $600,000 in it and I've been wondering what to do with it. The sales rep helped the client reposition his assets into an IRA consisting of conservative assets, so the client could sleep better at night. Needless to say, this sales rep has overcome his reluctance to asking the question. He has stepped through his mental baby gate. He always asks the client about other retirement accounts now.

Our little dogs are not limited so much by the actual baby gates we installed, because we don't even need to latch them anymore. They are limited by the "baby gates" they have developed in their minds. They do not believe they can penetrate the baby gates because, as puppies, they couldn't. In reality, today all they would need to do is push against the gates and their whole world would expand.

The same is true of all of us. Something in our minds blocks some of our activities. We didn't have success with an activity the first couple of times we tried it, and it became uncomfortable to continue doing it. So we don't try it anymore. Maybe our own business or personal worlds would expand, too, if we just tried to do the activity again. Maybe we only need to try it a couple more times, like Bill Harris's sales rep. You owe it to yourself to take a chance! PUSH THROUGH YOUR PERSONAL "BABY GATES!" YOU MIGHT BE AMAZED AT WHAT YOU DISCOVER. YOUR BUSINESS AND PERSONAL WORLDS WILL PROBABLY EXPAND BEYOND REALMS YOU NEVER EVEN CONCEIVED!

www.ingramcontent.com/pod-product-compliance
Lightning Source LLC
Chambersburg PA
CBHW021422170526
45164CB00001B/61